2 ∞
—
2 10f

ALSO BY

Carl L. Becker

Political Parties in the Province of New York from
1766–75 (1908)
Beginnings of the American People (1915)
Eve of the Revolution (1918)
Our Great Experiment in Democracy (1924)
The Declaration of Independence — A Study in the
History of Political Ideas (1922, 1942)
The Spirit of '76 *(with G. M. Clark and W. E. Dodd)*
(1926)
Modern History (1931)
The Heavenly City of the Eighteenth Century Phi-
losophers (1932)
Every Man His Own Historian (1935)
Progress and Power (1936)
Story of Civilization *(with Frederic Duncalf)* (1938)
Modern Democracy (1941)
New Liberties for Old (1941)

How New
Will the Better World Be?

HOW *NEW*

WILL THE BETTER

WORLD BE?

A discussion of Post-War Reconstruction

by CARL L. BECKER

Professor Emeritus of History in Cornell University

1944   *ALFRED A KNOPF*   New York

D
825
B38
1944

761 Buyers

83308

PUBLISHED MARCH 13, 1944

SECOND PRINTING, APRIL 1944

THIRD PRINTING, APRIL 1944

Published simultaneously in Canada by The Ryerson Press

SOCIETY *is indeed a contract. . . . But the state ought not to be considered as nothing better than a partnership agreement . . . to be taken up for a little temporary interest, and to be dissolved by the fancy of the parties. . . . It is a partnership in all science; a partnership in all art; a partnership in every virtue, and in all perfection. And as the ends of such a partnership cannot be obtained in many generations, it becomes a partnership not only between those who are living, but between those who are living, those who are dead, and those who are to be born.*

EDMUND BURKE

Preface

THE MARCH (Spring) number of the *Yale Review* for 1942 contained an article of mine, entitled "Making Democracy Safe in the World," which discussed certain aspects of what is called post-war reconstruction. A second article on the same general subject, entitled "How New Will the Better World Be?" appeared in the *Review* for March 1943. I was led to write these two articles because it seemed to me that the war had created a widespread state of mind very similar to that which prevailed during the last war — a feeling that the defeat of the Axis powers would provide us with an unprecedented opportunity to cure the international ills which made such wars possible. It is obvious of course that the present war, like the last one, is somehow associated with those complex forces which we denote by the terms "nationalism," "sovereign state," "power politics," and "imperialism." And since this is so, many people are saying that what we have to do to make a new and better world is to "abate nationalism, curb the sovereign state, abandon power politics, and end imperialism." Maybe so. But if so, then I think we have an impossible job on our hands. I quite agree that if something better than the inept pre-war policies and practices is not devised after the war, we shall be in for a very bad time indeed; but I think that it is quite futile to discuss post-war reconstruction on the assumption that the sentiment of nationalism will be any less strong than it has been, or that nations will cherish their sovereign independence any less than they have, or be less disposed to defend and promote their real or supposed national interests, or be less concerned with a balance of power that is advantageous to them. The two articles were written to suggest that these complex forces are the political realities of our time, and that they cannot be got rid of by wishing, or good resolutions, or treaties solemnly subscribed to.

The two articles, and especially the second one, called forth an unusual number of letters of commendation. Almost without exception the authors of the letters commended the articles for their "realism," and wanted to know where additional copies could be had. Partly for this reason I have now expanded the substance of the two articles into a short book. Besides, the articles were rather more concerned with what could not than with what could be done; and in the last two chapters of the book I have attempted to indicate some of the specific problems, more particularly certain economic problems, which will have to be in some measure solved if there is to be any new and better world. With the permission of the editors of the *Yale Review,* I have used the title of the second article as the title of the book. Perhaps I ought to add that the book would probably not have been written if Mr. Knopf had not, for some years past, exercised his gentle art of friendly but persistent prodding, in the belief apparently that it would be a good thing for all concerned if I would write a book for him on some subject of wide current interest.

C. B.

Ithaca, N.Y.
  October 1943

Contents

Contents

How NEW
Will the Better World Be?

1

What Is Wrong with the World We Have?

WHEN THE present war broke out in 1939 it seemed to most people incredible, just as it did in 1914, that such a disaster could occur in a world that was supposed to be highly civilized; and people were then everywhere asking: What could and should have been done to prevent it? But now, since it seems certain that the Axis powers will be defeated in the end, people are everywhere asking: What can and must be done after the war is over to prevent another such disaster occurring in another twenty-five years?

There are still some people who say that the only important thing now is to win the war, and that it is a waste of time and effort to talk about what can be done after it is won. But most people — at least most people who express their opinion — seem to think that the United Nations ought to get together now and agree on some plan or policy for dealing with the international problems that will arise as soon as Germany and Japan are defeated. This question — the question of "post-war reconstruction," as it is called — is now almost as much discussed as the war itself. It is being discussed over the radio, in the newspapers, on lecture platforms, and in private conversation. A vast number of books and pamphlets on the subject have been published, and the number increases week by week; and the subject is being systematically studied by British government officials, by our own State Department, and by various organizations of private citizens. Many different and conflicting plans and suggestions for "post-war reconstruction" have already been made, and more will be made, all designed to accomplish the same object — to prevent a repetition of wars such as this and the last one. More than ever before people throughout the world are aware that civilization cannot survive many such exhibitions of human folly; and more than ever before people throughout the world are convinced, and are saying, that this time something serious and effective must be done to "make a new and better world." But if we are to make a new and better world the first and all-important question is: What is wrong with the world we have, or the one we had before 1939, or before 1914?

1

Anyone can at any time point out any number of things that are wrong with the world. But just now it must be only too clear to everyone that the worst wrong thing with our world is war. War has always been one of the worst wrong things; and for more than two thousand years it has been well enough known to be so. What astounds and dismays us is that, knowing so well that war is wrong, and fearing and hating it more than anything else, we seem forced, in spite of ourselves, to go on waging it. And this is the more dismaying because we think, or did until 1914, that our world has become too highly civilized to tolerate anything so foolish. This is why the war of 1914 came to most people in this country, and even in Europe, as a complete surprise. It is true there were warnings enough for those who could read the signs; but in July 1914 most people felt that the world — the European world at least — was too civilized, too intelligent and humane, to permit such a disaster as a general war under modern conditions would surely prove to be. Up to the last minute most people felt that war would be avoided, as it had been in the two previous "crises" of 1905 and 1911; or at least that it would be "localized," confined to Austria and Serbia. And even after all the great powers were involved most people clung to the belief that, on account of the tremendous cost, such a war could not last more than six months or a year. But the war lasted four years and proved to be more widespread, more costly, and more ruthless and destructive than any war of equal length in the history of the world.

As the war went on year after year, the whole thing seemed incredible, a kind of nightmare without end. More and more people asked: Will this war prove to be the end of our civilization? More and more people said: Another war like it surely will. The general feeling was that "this must never happen again"; and in 1919 the League of Nations was established to make sure that it never would. Nevertheless, exactly twenty years after the League was established, it did happen again; and the present war has proved to be even more widespread, more costly, more ruthless and destructive, and will undoubtedly last longer than the last one.

No one is now saying, as so many people were in 1914, that we are too civilized to permit war. We are more inclined to say that a world in which such wars can happen cannot, after all, claim to be highly civilized. But that such wars can happen in our world still seems incredible; and we cling to the fact, and it is a fact, that we have the knowledge and power which, if they could be properly used, would enable us to create a far better civilization than it was ever possible to create before. Never before have men in fact used their knowledge and power to such good advantage in so many ways — for the mass production of the necessities and luxuries of life, for the increase of knowledge and the promotion of general education, for the prevention and cure of disease, for the abolition of famine and pestilence, for making life easy and comfortable and free from fear and want for so many people. In short, we live in a world that has the knowledge and power to create wealth, preserve life, and promote human welfare on a scale that was never before possible; and yet we live in a world in which, for eight years out of thirty-nine, men have in fact used this knowledge and power for death and destruction on a scale never before known.

This is the world we have, the world we live in. To ask whether it is or is not highly civilized does not help any. Whatever we call it, there is clearly something wrong with it; and the most obvious thing that is wrong with it is that it contains within it the conditions that have made possible two "global" and suicidal wars within the brief span of one generation.

War is, then, the first and worst thing that is wrong with our world. The second thing that is wrong is best known as "unemployment." It is more than that, but for the present let us call it that. For the present it is enough to note that these two wrong things — war and

6

unemployment — are related to each other in a very curious way. Unemployment troubles us only when we are at peace; when we wage total war it disappears.

In 1929 there occurred what is called the Great Depression. At that time a good lady said: "What a pity this old depression had to come just when times are so bad!" Times were indeed very bad. Stocks suddenly dropped until they were nearly worthless, banks and business enterprises failed, millions of men lost their jobs, and other millions of young men, wanting work and looking for jobs, could not find any. The same thing happened in all other industrialized countries — Germany, Italy, France, Belgium, Holland, and England. In Germany there were about six million unemployed, in England three or four, in the United States nearly ten. The depression was not only widespread, it lasted longer than similar depressions in the past. For ten years the great problem was how to get rid of unemployment, how to set business on its feet again, how to create jobs for men who desperately needed them. In England and the United States unemployed men were supported by private charity and government aid on a grand scale; and in both countries the government adopted various measures (in this country called the "New Deal") for aiding farmers and business men, and for creating jobs by building, at government expense, roads, houses, power dams, and the like. All of these measures helped, but they did not suffice to end unemployment.

Then Hitler, when he came to power in 1933, found an easier and quicker way to get rid of unemployment. He said that Germany needed guns more than it needed butter, and began to prepare for war. He built

7

up a great army, put the industrial plants to work at top speed and full time making war planes, submarines, tanks and trucks, guns and ammunition, military roads, arsenals, and aviation fields. In short, he devoted all the energies of the people to creating the means of death and destruction. And as soon as he did this, unemployment began to disappear, and in a few years there were no men without jobs in Germany. Then in 1939, being fully prepared, he began the war. England and France were involved; and as soon as they devoted all of their energies to the business of war, unemployment disappeared in those countries also. And as soon as the United States began to create a large army and to make arms and ammunition for it, and for supplying Great Britain, there was less unemployment in this country; and now that we are in the war everyone has a job, so that it is difficult to get a hired girl to work in the kitchen or an old man to mow the lawn.

Thus it seems that we live in a world so ordered that in peacetime millions of men are out of work, and they and their families lack food and clothes and other necessities of life. But as soon as war comes, all of these unemployed men find jobs, and when the war becomes "total" the problem is not how to find work for idle men, but where to find men enough for the work that needs to be done. We seem to live in a world in which the easiest and quickest way to abolish one wrong thing — unemployment and want — is to practice on a grand scale another wrong thing — war. It is surely a curiously ordered world in which we can abolish one serious evil only by creating another and worse one.

Is this, then, the only choice? Must we have either

unemployment and want, or war and destruction? It looks as if we must unless we can find some cure for these two wrong things. Curing them is the twofold problem of our time. These two problems are not new problems. There have always been unemployment and want within countries, and there have always been war and fear between them. The dismaying thing is that both of these evils seem to be worse than they ever were. Never before, or not for two hundred years, have unemployment and want, during so long a time, in so many countries with every means for creating wealth in abundance, reached the proportions of a major social disaster. Never before has war been so nearly "global," so nearly "total," so ruthlessly brutal and disastrous as to threaten the destruction of civilization. What we need to know, then, is why it is that in our time, when we have at last acquired the knowledge and power which, if properly applied, are capable of abolishing the two evils — fear and want, war and unemployment — these two evils are becoming worse instead of better.

2

The explanation of this curious situation is to be found chiefly in what is called the Industrial or, better still, the Technological Revolution — that is to say, the changes that have been brought about in the last two hundred years by the discovery of steam power, electricity, and radiation, the progress of natural science, and the consequent invention of the innumerable implements and appliances and complicated and powerful machines with which everyone is familiar. This was one of the three or four most important revolutions in the history of man, the most important perhaps since the invention of the art of writing, some five thousand years ago. The most general result of this revolution was to give men a power to control and manipulate material things never dreamed of before, and thereby to change in a comparatively short time the old ways of living and making a living, of raising food and manufacturing commodities, of travel and transportation of goods, and of sending news and information from one place to another. But the revolution had two particular results that have much to do with the subject we are considering — unemployment and war. One of these is that men do less of the work and machines do more of it than formerly; the other is that the lives and fortunes of people in any community or country are affected more than formerly, for good or ill, by what people in other communities or countries are doing or may do.

Men do less of the work and machines do more. Two hundred or even one hundred years ago a good many men had to work a long time to print a small book. The type for each letter had to be set by hand. The man who set the type, perched on a stool, had in front of him, raised at an angle of forty-five degrees, a frame of little compartments, one compartment containing all the "a" type, another all the "b" type, and so on. Printing a book in this way was a slow business — so slow that one man could copy a manuscript in longhand more quickly than two or three men could print it.

Now all that has been completely changed. A few years ago I visited the plant where the Stanford University Press prints its books. In a small room a press was running out the signatures that would be bound in a volume. The press was a complicated, although not a very large machine — maybe six feet wide and eight feet high at the highest end; and to say that it was "running out the signatures" is quite correct. For all I could see of its delicate and complicated activity was, at one end a broad sheet of blank white paper being rapidly drawn in between two rollers, and at the other end printed and neatly folded signatures being ejected and expertly piled one on top of another. There was only one man in the room. The point is that the one machine, with one man to run it, did in one day the work which would formerly have required the labor of many men working many days. And so in all industries: as machines become more complicated and automatic, fewer men are required to run them.

This gives rise to what the economists call "technological unemployment." When a job is taken over by a machine, the man who formerly did the job and got paid for it is out of luck — he is no longer needed for that job. In the early nineteenth century the workers in England realized that the new machines for making cotton cloth were throwing them out of work, and crowds of unemployed men often broke into the factories and smashed up the machines. The advance in technology had left them unemployed. Now if, with the coming of the machines for making cotton cloth, no more cotton cloth had been made than formerly, technological unemployment would have been more serious than it was — it would have been chronic and disastrous. But since the new machines could make in a month or a year far more cotton cloth than was possible by the old methods, a great deal more was made.

More and more factories were established to make cotton cloth, not only for the people of England, but for the people of other countries as well. In 1913 the mills of Great Britain made several billion yards of cotton cloth for export alone. And so it happened that in 1913, although the machines did most of the work of making cotton cloth, so much of it was made that there were far more jobs in the cotton industry than there had been in the eighteenth century, when most of the work was done by men. Thus technological unemployment may not be serious as long as an industry is *expanding* — making more and more of the same thing: the expanding industry creates new jobs to take the place of those which the machines have destroyed.

The machines may create new jobs in another way — by creating new industries. Perhaps the best example is the automobile. In 1900 the new "horseless carriage" was generally regarded as a kind of stunt contraption, an amusing fad for rich people. But very soon certain persons realized that it was bound to become an essential means of travel and transportation. One of these persons was Henry Ford, who set out to make an automobile cheap enough so that most families in the United States could have one. Making automobiles for rich and poor thus became one of the great industries of the United States; and the tremendous expansion of this business provided employment for many thousands of men — created new jobs that had not existed before. Besides, the automobile created new industries. To build better and better automobiles new and more complicated machines were required; and the making of machines to make the automobile was a new industry, providing more jobs. And as the number of automobiles increased, more and more rubber and gasoline were needed; and so there was an expansion of the gasoline and rubber business, and more jobs still.

An expanding industry thus takes up unemployed men by creating new jobs, and a new invention may create a new industry which in turn creates other new industries, all of which create still more new jobs. But there are limits to the expansion of any industry, and to the expansion of all the industries of a country at any time.

These limits are ultimately set by the extent of the market — the number of people willing and able to buy the commodities offered at the price asked. Manufacturers of cotton cloth or automobiles must dispose of their products at a price that nets them a profit; and as long as they can find additional buyers at that price they can go on enlarging their factories and employing more men. For many years Henry Ford could sell as many Ford cars as he could make, because he had a new, untapped market — all the people in the United States who wanted and could afford a cheap car. But when most of these people had cheap cars the market was more limited.

The market was further limited by competition from the manufacturers of other cheap cars. Such competition Mr. Ford could meet in one of two ways: either by cutting cost of production and improving the car while selling it at the same or a lower price, or by a more efficient "sales policy" — better advertising, more pressure on dealers to dispose of more cars — which would induce people to buy a Ford car rather than some other. Cutting the cost of production could be done by "mass production," standardizing the parts, and especially by devising better and more automatic machines which could do more of the work with fewer laborers. Wages paid to laborers were always a good part of the cost of production, so that anything which reduced the number of laborers, lengthened their hours of work, or cut their wages would cut cost of production and enable the manufacturer to keep the price down and extend the market. But then, if there are throughout the country fewer laborers employed, or if their wages are cut, the laboring classes will be less able to buy the product of the manufacturers, and so the market will to that extent be curtailed.

Taking the industries of a country as a whole, managers and employers of labor are confronted with a conflict of interest which is extremely difficult to reconcile. As makers of goods to be sold at as low a price as possible, it is to their individual interest to employ as few men as possible and pay them as low wages as possible; but as sellers of goods it is to their interest, individually and collectively, to have throughout the country as many men as possible working at high wages, so that there will be as many people as possible able to buy their goods. This is the central problem created by machine mass production and the price system: how to keep costs and prices down so that everyone will be eager to buy, and at the same time keep everyone employed at good wages so that everyone will be able to buy.

This difficulty becomes greatest at those times when, for a great variety of reasons, the market becomes too restricted — when all avenues for "expansion" seem

14

closed. Then there is a condition of "overproduction"
— more of the commodities already produced than
can be sold. In that case production has to be cut down
— factories running on part time, fewer laborers
needed, men discharged, and consequently "unemployment." If the situation is general — if it involves
all the chief industries of the country — there is a
"business crisis," a "general depression"; in short,
plenty of commodities, plenty of people needing commodities, but not enough "purchasing power," not
enough people working at good wages to buy the commodities. With fewer people buying, prices fall and
profits decline, so that the manufacturers have to cut
costs still more by reducing wages or discharging more
men, thus still further reducing the number of people
with money to buy.

Such "crises" or "depressions" have occurred at
more or less regular intervals during the last hundred
and fifty years. They usually lasted only a few years,
and although they created hardship and unemployment they did not reach the proportions of a national
disaster. The last of these crises was the Great Depression of 1929, which lasted longer, was more widespread, and affected more people than any previous
crisis. It was so bad that for years some ten million
men were unemployed. They and their families had to
be supported by federal and state "relief." So many
banks failed that President Roosevelt closed them
all for a few days, until they could be supplied with
sufficient deposits to meet their obligations. Farmers
and manufacturers could escape bankruptcy only by
cutting down production still further, and thereby
throwing more laborers on relief. Machine mass pro-

duction had, in short, resulted in a situation which, however tragic, was inherently absurd — a situation in which "overproduction" was causing widespread want. In a country of plenty, or capable of producing plenty, millions of people were in need of food and clothes and other necessities of life, and yet the only way under the price system to keep farmers from starving seemed to be to plow cotton underground and limit the production of wheat and corn.

3

Thus one effect of the Technological Revolution — the coming of the machines — has been mass production, nation-wide or world-wide markets, business crises that become more widespread and severe, and mass unemployment that reaches the proportions of national disaster. But the coming of the machines has had another effect, which is closely related to the first one. It has given us means of rapid communication and transportation that have made the world, as we say, a "small place." Mr. Willkie has expressed this fact in the title of his book — *One World*. In many ways it is not one world — for example, in government, in language, in religion. But more and more it is becoming one world economically, which means that more and more the economic interests and activities of the people of any community or country are affected, for good or ill, by the economic interests and activities of people in other communities and countries. And this is why business crises and mass unemployment and wars tend to become more widespread and more disastrous.

This process of becoming "one world" has been going on for a very long time, but only recently has it reached the point of being revolutionary in its effects. Even as late as the eighteenth century the relation between communities and countries was far less close and far less important than it is now. In the eighteenth century the people of any country, or of any small community within a country, could go their own way without bothering too much about what happened in other communities or countries. In any small community the people for the most part raised their own food, made their own clothes, managed their own small business enterprises with their own money and their own labor, and disposed of the things they had to sell within the immediate neighborhood. A man who made hats needed little capital. Such little as he might lack he borrowed of his neighbors or the local bank. His advertising was confined to a line in the local newspaper: "John Smith, hatter, Elm Street." He sold his hats to people in the community, not throughout the country. If there was a dispute between an employer and his laborers in Philadelphia, that did not matter to anyone else in the town, still less to the people who lived in New York. There was a certain amount of trade between communities and between countries, and such trade might be highly profitable to those engaged in it; but if the trade of any community or country had been suddenly cut off, it would have been, although a serious matter to many people, not a disaster for the community or the country as a whole.

Now all that has been changed. Machine mass production, rapid transportation and communication, and nation-wide and world-wide markets have created a situation in which neither communities nor countries can safely live in "isolation." A few years ago there was a strike in the Chrysler automobile plant at Detroit which lasted nearly two months, so that during that time no Chrysler, Dodge, or Plymouth cars were made. Legally the strike was a dispute between the laborers and the employers in a private industry in Detroit and did not concern anyone else; but in fact the strike did concern many other people. It affected the business interests or customary activities of many people throughout the country — people who had nothing to do with bringing on the strike and could do nothing to end it. In theory the Chrysler enterprise was a private business run for private profit, but in fact it was in some sense a public utility. In the case of larger enterprises, supplying more essential goods or services, this is still more true — for example, the telephone, the telegraph, the railroads. If a strike should tie up the New York Central and Pennsylvania Railroads for two months, the result would be too disastrous to be tolerated. The government would have to interfere, and say to the owners in effect: "You are not merely the owners of a private business run for private profit; you are public servants managing a public utility, and the public interest demands that your railroads shall be kept running."

It is not only the communities of a single country that are thus drawn together by machine mass production and expanding markets; the countries of the world are, to a less extent, similarly drawn together. Ford cars are sold in nearly every country. The Standard Oil Company of New Jersey is active in every country where oil can be sold, and in every spot on the globe where rich deposits of oil have been or may be found. All highly industrialized countries produce

18

more than they can consume. The surplus must be sold in other countries. The business enterprises interested in exports seek markets wherever they can be found, and new opportunities for business enterprise wherever there is the best prospect of high profit. In all highly industrialized countries "capital" — that is, money — accumulates in banks; and capital, wanting as it were to be invested, flows inevitably, as water runs downhill, into those parts of the world where the highest return is to be obtained. All industrialized countries need certain essential raw materials, such as oil and rubber, coal and iron, some of which are to be had within the country itself, but not all, so that it is necessary for the country to obtain what is lacking either by trading with or controlling the countries where it is to be found.

As a result of this situation there was, from about 1860 to the end of the nineteenth century, a very rapid expansion of European and American capital and business enterprise into the so-called "backward" countries of the world — Africa, the Near East, China, and the East Indies. The expansion of capital and business enterprise was inevitably followed by political intervention and control of one sort or another. Africa was partitioned between the principal European countries. Russia and Great Britain obtained "spheres of influence" in Persia. France obtained Indo-China, Germany obtained special rights in the rich Chinese province of Shantung, and the chief European countries and the United States obtained special rights in the principal Chinese ports.

Until the end of the nineteenth century this scramble for control of the "backward countries" went on without giving rise to serious trouble or much comment. But then (1898–1904) there occurred in rapid succession a number of "little colonial wars" — the Boer War, the Spanish-American War, the "Boxer Rebellion" in China, the Russo-Japanese War. These little colonial wars were the prelude to more serious conflicts. To defend their common interests against the Triple Alliance of Germany, Austro-Hungary, and Italy, Great Britain, France, and Russia united in the Triple Entente; and between 1905 and 1914 several "diplomatic crises" occurred, growing out of the German-French conflict of interest in Morocco, and Russian-Austrian conflict of interest in the Balkans and Turkey. The last of these crises resulted in World War I, which was the first act in the world tragedy of which the present war is the second.

4

War and mass unemployment are, then, two principal — although by no means the only — things that are wrong with our world. It would of course be a great mistake to think that either of these evils is the result of simple causes. But it is clear that mass unemployment is in great part caused by the failure of our economic system to get the goods that are or can be produced properly distributed among the people who need them; and that this and the last war were caused in great part by the competitive struggle of the great industrial countries for the trade and raw materials of the world. The Atlantic Charter recognizes this fact. It states that when the war is over, one of the aims of the United Nations will be "to bring about . . . in the economic field . . . improved labor standards, economic adjustments, and social security"; and that another aim will be "to further the enjoyment by all states, great and small, victor or vanquished, of access, on equal terms, to the trade and raw materials of the world which are necessary for their prosperity." To do these two things would be to do much to make a better world.

But to do either of these things will be extremely difficult — much more difficult than many people now appear to think it will be. Our thinking is now somewhat distorted by what is called "war psychology." While fighting such a war as this we are all apt to think that the all-important thing is to win the war — and that is right enough; but we are also apt to think that nothing can be so hard as war, and that when the war is won anything that needs then to be done will be much easier. This state of mind, this "war psychology," leads to two mistaken notions. One is that the war will have taught us a needed lesson, and that when it is over we shall somehow be much wiser and more humane, so that we shall be able to make a "new world" entirely. The other is that when the war is won our real difficulties will be over, and that we can then return to the relatively good times before the war occurred.

Of these two mistaken notions, the idea that we can return to "normalcy" is the most dangerous, because it will prove to be the most serious obstacle to making a better world, to say nothing of a new world. First of all, therefore, let us consider why it is impossible to return to normalcy.

2

Can We Return to Normalcy?

AT ALL TIMES in the history of civilization the conditions of life for the majority of men have been harsh
or unsatisfactory, and at all times men have therefore
found compensation for the immediate present by
dreaming of a better world that has existed or may or
might exist at some other time or place. The ancient
Greeks dreamed of a Golden Age of the remote past,
at the beginning of created things, when, as Hesiod
says, "men lived like gods, free from toil and grief."
The early Christians dreamed of a Golden Age of the
remote future, when Christ would come again and establish the Church Triumphant, in which peace and
justice would reign. But our credulity is not sufficiently
robust to give even a semblance of reality to either the
beginning or the end of created things, and we have
therefore to be content with a Golden Age of a less
remote past or future — the Golden Age of the social
revolution which our grandchildren will enjoy, or the
Golden Age of the horse-and-buggy days which our
grandfathers knew.

The disposition to look back to "the good old days"
and the desire to have them come again is deeply em-
bedded in most of us — especially as we grow older.
Young people are more apt to welcome change since
their habits of thinking and acting are less settled. We

are therefore often startled, and even dismayed, to find our children thinking strange thoughts and doing strange things, so that any father is often moved to say to his son: "When you are as old as I am you'll know better." And the son is apt to think, even if he does not say: "I surely will."

So far as this conflict is one between fathers and sons, it isn't very serious — it is merely a domestic, not a social problem. But in times of rapid social and economic changes the conflict becomes more serious: it becomes a conflict between those whose interests are, or seem to them to be, best served by resisting the changes and preserving the old ways, and those whose interests are, or seem to them to be, best served by accepting the new ways. We are now living in such a time — a time of uncommonly rapid change in the conditions of living. The last war and the present one were caused in great part by these changes; but the last war was, and the present one will be, itself the cause of further and more rapid changes. The great need of our time, therefore, is to adjust our habits of thought and conduct to these rapid changes, so that we can live in the world as it is with the least amount of strain and frustration.

That is the great need, but that is also the great difficulty. It is extremely difficult to change fixed habits, and still more difficult to change fixed ideas, as rapidly as the changing conditions of life demand. The result is that our ideas are usually "behind the times." It is often said of military men that they "are always fighting the last war" — fighting the present war according to ideas about war which they acquired in the preceding war when the conditions of fighting were very dif-

23

ferent. Military men are not alone in this. Most of us are apt to be fighting social and international problems with obsolete ideas — attempting to solve social and international problems by means of ideas which were good enough at an earlier time when the problems were quite different.

This "cultural lag" — this lagging behind of ideas in a changing social world — is always the chief obstacle to making a new and better world. It is especially so now when we are in the midst of a war as revolutionary as this one is sure to be. We all think of the war as a catastrophe — which it is. But we are apt to think of it also as a temporary *interruption* of our ordinary life. During the war we are willing to make sacrifices, and are easily persuaded that after the war is over something will be done — something in general — to make the sacrifices worth while. But when the war is over, most people will be so glad that it is over and done with that they will wish not to have to think about it any more. Their strongest desire will be to return to the occupations and interests which, on account of the war, they have had to give up for the time being.

1

In this country the desire to return to what are regarded as "normal" conditions will probably be stronger in respect to international than in respect to national affairs. Some months ago a representative of *Time* magazine interviewed some American soldiers home from the front on leave. What did they think of the war? All of them thought that the people back home failed to realize how serious the war was or what it was like — naturally enough, since no one could

24

who had not been at the front. All of them were convinced that we were up against something really
tough, and that we had to get tough enough to finish
up the business and do a complete job of it. But one of
them added that when the war was won and he got
back to the U.S.A. he "never wanted to hear of a foreign country again."

In expressing his own feeling, the soldier expressed
a feeling that is more or less instinctive with the great
majority of people in the United States. They have
always had the fixed idea that "foreign countries" —
meaning European countries chiefly; China and India are too remote and strange to count — are well
enough in their way, no doubt, but that we needn't
have much to do with them. During the nineteenth
century this attitude was more or less justified, and
became fixed, because it was in accord with the facts
of geography and world politics. It was also in accord
with the established political policy of the government. As early as 1776 Thomas Paine, in his famous
pamphlet *Common Sense,* advocated separation from
Great Britain on the ground that political union with
Great Britain had always involved us in European
wars — wars which we had done nothing to bring
about and from which we derived no benefit. For the
same reason Washington, in his Farewell Address, ad-
vised the people of the United States not to become
involved in European political rivalries; and for the
same reason Thomas Jefferson, in his first Inaugural
Address, laid down the principle: "Peace, commerce
and honest friendship with all nations, entangling alliances with none."

This principle became the basis of our foreign policy

— a policy of "isolation" — during the nineteenth century. We would not meddle with European affairs so long as European countries did not meddle with American affairs. We would of course defend our rights. Twice only during the nineteenth century were we thus forced, as we thought, to defend our rights — against England in 1812, and against Spain in 1898. But all such interventions in European affairs were thought to be temporary interruptions of the normal policy and procedure, to which we expected as a matter of course to return as soon as the rights were vindicated.

When the World War I broke out in 1914 this policy of isolation, of no entangling alliances, was followed by President Wilson. He at once proclaimed that the United States would remain neutral, and he even went so far as to say that the people should be neutral in "thought" as well as in deed. The proclamation of neutrality was generally approved. But the statement that we should all be neutral in thought as well as in deed was widely resented, because most people were not, and could not be, neutral in thought. On the contrary, the great majority of the people sympathized with Great Britain and France and hoped they would win the war. As the war went on, this feeling became stronger, especially in the Eastern states; and by 1916 many people, perhaps a majority, were convinced that if the war dragged on much longer the United States would be drawn into it. Some were eager for that event, some only resigned to it; but the general opinion was coming to be that it would be necessary.

For this change of opinion there were many reasons.

One was the belief that England and France were fighting in defense of democracy, while Germany was fighting in defense of "autocracy." Another was that since Germany was out to dominate the world, we would have to fight her some time, and that it was better to do it now with the aid of Great Britain and France than to wait until they were defeated and then have to do it alone. But what actually brought us into the war was German violation of our neutral rights by submarine warfare. No single thing did so much to overcome our desire to stay out of the war as the sinking of the *Lusitania;* and the specific reason for declaring war was Germany's refusal to abandon "unrestricted" submarine warfare. This was in accord with long-established governmental policy and the settled ideas of the people; and when we entered the war the great majority of the people felt as they always had done — that we must first win the war and then withdraw from European affairs and mind our own business.

So the great majority felt. But for some time a good many people had been thinking that the United States ought to take a more active part in world affairs. As early as the Spanish-American War in 1898 a new term was coined — "world power." It was said that we were, after all, a world power like Great Britain, and should therefore play our proper part in world politics. And indeed from that time the United States did take a somewhat more active part in world affairs. In 1900 it took part in suppressing the Boxer Rebellion in China; in 1905 it took part in the Algeciras Conference, called to settle the German-French conflict in Morocco. In 1899 and 1907 it took part in the Hague

Conferences, called to consider disarmament and resulting in the creation of the Hague Tribunal; and on the eve of the first World War many people, including ex-President Taft, were actively promoting a project for a League to Enforce Peace.

The man who above all others gave force and direction to this new idea was Woodrow Wilson. Before we entered the war in 1917 he informed France and Great Britain that if they were fighting merely to change the balance of power, grab the German colonies, and partition the Turkish Empire, the United States was not interested. But if they were fighting to make a just and lasting peace — if they were really fighting a "war to end war," a war to "make the world safe for democracy" — the United States would be very much interested in that. To make his position clear, he formulated the Fourteen Points as the "war aims" of the United States and the basis of a just and lasting peace. The main points were: (1) the right of all nations to govern themselves; (2) the right of all nations to free "navigation upon the seas"; (3) the right of all nations "consenting to the peace" to "equality of trade conditions"; (4) agreement of all nations that "armaments will be reduced to the lowest point consistent with domestic safety"; and (5) the formation of a League of Nations to prevent war by guaranteeing "political and territorial integrity to great and small nations alike." This was Woodrow Wilson's program for making a new and better world, and he was convinced that the people of the world, including the people of the United States, would support it.

But the people of the United States did not support Wilson or his program. Why did they not? Some have said that Wilson himself was to blame, that his mistake was to have gone to the Peace Conference at all; others have said that, having decided to go to the conference, his mistake was not to have taken some prominent members of the Republican Party, such as Elihu Root or ex-President Taft. But his great mistake was not to have foreseen that the "war psychology" would give way to a "peace psychology." He failed to foresee that when Germany was defeated, the fear of Germany, which had united the Allied Nations during the war and generated the emotional idealism necessary to sustain the war effort, would disappear, and thus leave individuals and nations free to revert to their customary peacetime habits of thought and to pursue their customary peacetime interests.

This at all events is what happened. At the Peace Conference Wilson was dismayed to find that the "plain people everywhere" deserted him. When he appealed to them over the heads of their governments they denounced him. Statues formerly erected in his honor were removed or destroyed. His popularity and power rapidly waned, and although he got a better peace than would have been made without him, he felt that he had failed to get the "just and lasting peace" which he had expected to get. His one consolation was that he got what he most wanted and thought most important — the League of Nations. But when he returned from Paris he found that even the people of the United States refused to support him. The Senate refused to sanction his promise that the United States would join the League; and in the election of 1920 his people virtually repudiated him and his policies by returning, with a sweeping majority,

the Republican Party to power and electing Warren
G. Harding as President.

The election of Harding, a muddle-minded man
devoid of ability, force, or distinction, was the result
of many and complex influences. But what it meant
above all was that the great majority of the people of
the United States were determined, now that the war
was over, to withdraw from the affairs of Europe. It
meant that they were fed up with Europe and its problems, fed up with hearing about them, and fed up even
with Woodrow Wilson and his noble ideals. The general reversion from the heroic to the ordinary level
of living President Harding was eminently capable of
expressing instinctively, without taking thought further than to consult a dictionary. He expressed it by
saying that now, happily, the people of the United
States could "return to normalcy."

2

In saying that the people of the United States could
return to normalcy Harding meant chiefly that they
had had enough of Wilson's effort to lead them on a
crusade to reform international affairs. But he meant
more than that. He meant that the people had also had
enough of Wilson's effort to lead the country on a
crusade to reform the economic and social system of
the United States. During his first administration
(1912–16) Wilson had formulated and partly carried
through a broad program of social reform, which he
called the "New Freedom." The New Freedom was
itself the outcome of what was known as the "Progressive movement" — a movement that had been going
on for some twenty years, designed to correct many ob-

vious abuses that had developed more or less un-checked since the Civil War. What was this Progressive movement or New Freedom which in 1921 President Harding thought the people had had enough of?

When the Civil War ended, in 1865, the people of the victorious North were glad enough to return to normalcy. They too, like the people of 1921, had had enough of public affairs, of heroic living and noble ideals. For these and other reasons the period follow-ing the Civil War was not the time in our history of which we can be most proud. It was a time of rapid industrial and technological development, rapid in-crease in the production of wealth, phenomenal growth of private fortunes, the accumulation of money in banks, and, above all, the concentration of wealth and economic power in the hands of great corporations — the Standard Oil Company, the Carnegie Steel Cor-poration, the International Harvester Company, the Pullman Company, and many others. It was also an age characterized by the close connection between politics and "big business" — an age of ruthless com-petition and questionable business practices made easy by widespread political corruption that flourished too often under the indifference or with the connivance of mediocre political leaders.

Of this economic development the outstanding so-cial result was to create a conflict of interest between the few rich and the many poor — between big and little business, between industrial laborers and their employers, between farmers and the milling, packing, and railroad corporations, which, as they thought, kept down the price of farm products. In 1886 Andrew Car-negie, whose steel industry made him a multi-millionaire, published a book entitled *Triumphant Democracy,* in which he pointed out with satisfaction the marvelous progress in the production of wealth made under democratic government; but six years earlier Henry George had published a book entitled *Progress and Poverty,* in which he pointed out with dissatisfaction the startling fact that the marvelous progress in the production of wealth had been accomplished by widespread poverty for the mass of the people.

Henry George was more denounced than read because he advocated, as the only remedy, a single tax on private property in land. But the "plain people" were aware, especially in times of industrial "panics," that something was wrong and that something must be done about it. The panic of 1873 was followed by legislation in the Western states for regulating freight rates charged by railroads, and the courts upheld these laws on the ground that railroads were not merely private enterprises but in the nature of public utilities, and that "the State must be permitted to adopt such rules and regulations as may be necessary for the promotion of the general welfare of the people." In the early 1890's there occurred the "Populist" movement, strongest in Kansas, where the farmers were urged by Mary Lease to "raise less corn and more Hell." The depression of 1893 gave rise to the "free silver" movement, a movement for cheap money which would benefit the debtor classes. In 1896 the Democratic Party adopted the cause of free silver, and nominated as its candidate for president William J. Bryan. And in his famous "Cross of Gold" speech at Chicago Bryan expressed the essence of the social conflict which for twenty years had been gathering force. The conflict, he said, was one between the rich and powerful on the one side, and on the other "the producing masses of this nation, supported by the commercial interests, and the toilers everywhere."

Bryan was defeated, but he may be said to have given birth to the "Progressive movement" of the next twenty years. In the late 1890's writers of books and articles, newspaper editors, and prominent leaders in both parties denounced political corruption and the unfair practices of big business. In a series of brilliant articles in *McClures' Magazine* Lincoln Steffens exposed "the shame of the cities." In her *History of the Standard Oil Company* Ida Tarbell disclosed the methods by which that company had obtained a monopoly of the business. For such writers Theodore Roosevelt coined a phrase: he called them "muckrakers." But the force of public sentiment was such that he had to support the muck-rakers. He became the leader of the "Progressive movement," denounced "malefactors of great wealth," declared that there must be a " square deal" for all classes, and supported legislation directed against the trusts and in favor of the laboring classes.

It was said that Roosevelt had "stolen Bryan's clothes," which was true enough; and although the Progressive movement appeared to have spent its force during the Taft administration, it was revived by Woodrow Wilson in 1912. The object of his administration, Wilson said, would be to win a "New Freedom" for the people of the United States. "We must," he told the Congress, "abolish everything that bears even a semblance of privilege or any kind of artificial advantage." To that end a number of important meas-

33

ures were passed through Congress, the most important being the Federal Reserve Act (1913), which re-
organized and improved the federal system of banking
and currency; the Clayton Anti-Trust Act (1914), designed to curb the power of great corporations and to
improve the position of labor unions in bargaining
with employers; the Underwood Tariff Act (1913),
designed to promote international trade by lowering
the tariffs on imported goods; and the Sixteenth
Amendment, which made possible a graduated income tax.

The enactment of other measures contemplated by
the Wilson New Freedom program was prevented by
the entrance of the United States into the war in 1917,
and after the war the people were in a mood to re-
pudiate Wilson's policies both domestic and foreign
— the New Freedom as well as the League of Nations.
Under Harding they again tried the experiment of returning to normalcy.

The period of the 1920's was not, any more than the
period following the Civil War, a time in our history
of which anyone can be very proud. It was a time of
skepticism and disillusionment. So far from having
made the world safe for democracy, the war had only
intensified social and international conflicts. Young
people, having been promised a new and better world,
found only a worse one, and were therefore in a mood
to believe in nothing. Many of their elders, writers and
college professors, equally disillusioned, taught them
to place a low value on "ideals." The real motives of
men and nations, it was said, were always selfish, the
professed motives never sincere. Democratic govern-

ment, like any other, so it was said, was designed to benefit the few at the expense of the many. To imagine that men could become good or the world made better was a vain thing; to get yours while the going was good was the only wisdom. After 1925 the going was very good for a short and merry time. It was a "boom time," a time of frantic speculation and of fortunes made and lost overnight. Trusts were replaced by "holding companies" designed to side-step the anti-trust laws. The price of stocks rose to unprecedented heights, and it was widely believed that a new era had dawned — that American ingenuity and business efficiency had at last discovered the secret of permanent and universal prosperity.

This delirium suddenly ended in 1929. At the end of November the listed value of stocks in the United States was some forty billion dollars less than at the beginning of October. All prominent business men and political leaders, including President Hoover, assured the people that this was only a temporary setback. Everything, they said, pointed to a quick recovery; prosperity was "just around the corner." In fact the collapse proved to be more world-wide, more prolonged, and more disastrous than any previous one; and when Franklin D. Roosevelt was inaugurated as President in March 1933, so many banks were failing that it was necessary to close all the banks in the country until they could be provided with sufficient cash to meet the demands of their depositors and thus avoid complete financial and business chaos. Thus ended the experiment of returning to normalcy, and thus began the New Deal, which was nothing new at all, but merely a revival and an expansion of Theodore Roosevelt's Square Deal and Woodrow Wilson's New Freedom.

3

The return to normalcy proved to be even more disastrous in international than in national affairs. It is easy to see that now — easy to see how mistaken was the policy of isolation pursued by all the democratic countries up to the very eve of the present war. It is easy to see now that Great Britain, France, and the lesser democratic countries of Europe, by prompt, decisive, and united action, could have prevented the occupation of Austria, the rape of Czechoslovakia, and the destruction of Poland. It is easy to see now that it was to their interest to do so. It is easy to see that it would have been to the interest of the United States to have joined with them. In short, it is easy now to see that if, in the pre-war years, the democratic countries had placed a higher value on their freedom and independence than they did on the desire to return to normalcy and their fear of becoming involved in war, they could have prevented the war in which, one by one, as circumstances dictated, they are all now more or less disastrously involved. It is convenient, but not sensible, to place the responsibility upon "reactionary" governments (on Chamberlain and the Cliveden House set, on Daladier and the French Fascists) for adopting a policy of "appeasement." But the truth is that there was not, in any of these countries, on any of the crucial occasions, a sufficiently strong or united sentiment to support a policy which might have committed the country to the risk of war.

The policy of the United States was no different

36

from that of the democratic countries of Europe, and no less mistaken; but its fear of becoming involved in a European war and its determination to stay out were intensified by the widespread belief that it could and should have kept out of the last one. During the 1920's reliable historians, both European and American, investigating the causes of the war, reached the conclusion that Germany was not after all solely responsible for beginning it — not more responsible than France, and even less so than Russia. Accepting this conclusion, many popular writers in the United States presented the war and the peace from a more objective or even a more cynical point of view. The war, they said, was just another conflict between the great powers of Europe for territory and commercial advantage. Having won the war, the victorious countries proceeded according to plan to break up the Austro-Hungarian Monarchy and to partition the Turkish Empire; and, contrary to the Fourteen Points, they imposed on Germany cession of her colonies, disarmament, and indemnities that could not be paid.

If all of this was true, or even partly true, then it seemed that in entering the war in 1917 the United States had made a mistake, and a costly one. It had been a mistake to think that without our aid Great Britain and France would have been decisively defeated. Without our aid the war would have ended in a stalemate, and the peace would then have been a "negotiated" instead of a "dictated" peace, a "peace without victory," which Wilson himself had said was desirable; and that would have been better, because a compromise peace, not being all to the advantage of the Allied Nations, would have left Germany reasonably satisfied and too strong to be declared an out-cast and shoved around at the convenience of the victorious countries. So it was said and widely believed in the United States, and this view contributed to a feeling of resentment, a deep-seated suspicion that the United States had been dragged into the war without first finding out what the pay-off was.

So thinking, many people said that entering the war in 1917 was a case of bad judgment on our part, and let it go at that. Others looked for an excuse — blamed Wilson for bamboozling us with his fantastic idea of a "war to end war," or else said that we were maneuvered into the war by the sinister, undercover activities of the international bankers and munitions-makers to advance their selfish interests, or made out that we were a nation of simple, starry-eyed idealists, easily taken in by the skillful propaganda of the British and the French, who made use of us to pull their chestnuts out of the fire. And whether this was true, or only debatable, or merely preposterous, it was a fact that in 1934 the world was in a worse state than in 1914, and that the war, so far from having made the world safe for democracy, had made it convenient for dictators, and so far from having purged the world of all wars, had created conditions that threatened a new one.

In this state of mind the people of the United States watched the rise of Hitler and the establishment of the Nazi government with some interest but not much alarm; to them, as to many in Europe, Hitler seemed a conceited, comical fellow ranting nonsense. When he made good his boasts, they were still not much alarmed, nor had they any idea that the United States could or should do anything about it. If Hitler and Mussolini needed to be stopped, it was for the League of Nations or France and Great Britain to stop them. The United States was not, thank God, a member of the League; and since neither Great Britain nor France was willing to interfere, the United States could hardly be expected to. And after all, however little we might like the Nazi form of government, that was something for the Germans to take and like if they wanted to; and if Germany wanted an army, that was no more than any country was entitled to; and if Hitler wanted all German-speaking people united under a German government, that was in accord with the principle of "national self-determination," which Wilson had made so much of in the Fourteen Points. If Hitler went farther than that and precipitated another European war, Europe could take care of it; the United States would not again go on a crusade to set the world right.

Although determined to stay out of the war, the fear that we might be involved in spite of ourselves was nevertheless great. Declaring our neutrality would not necessarily prevent many grave "incidents," such as the sinking of the *Lusitania* in the last war. According to international law, a neutral state had certain duties and also certain rights. Its duty was not to give military aid to any of the warring countries, and not to trade with any of them in goods that were declared "contraband of war." But it had the right to carry on trade in all commodities with all neutral countries, and in all "neutral" commodities with the warring countries except in such ports as might be actually blockaded. These were our "neutral rights"; but if we exercised these rights, our ships sailing into the North

Sea and the English Channel might be sunk by German submarines; the loss of American lives and property would tend to create a warlike temper; and if Germany, in spite of diplomatic protests, kept on sinking our ships we might then, for all our good intentions, be forced to enter the war in defense of our neutral rights, just as we were in 1917.

This being so, the United States did a very strange thing, something it had never done before: it declined to exercise its neutral rights for fear that it might have to defend them. In effect it said to the warring powers: "Define for us those regions on the sea, those 'war zones,' where our ships are in danger of being sunk by submarines, and we will keep our ships and our citizens out of them. We will sell you our commodities, but we will not carry them in our ships. You must come and buy them here, and pay cash on the line, and carry them away in your own ships. As a neutral country our citizens have a right to travel on the sea and to carry on trade in neutral goods with all countries without being molested by the warring countries. Hitherto we have exercised these rights and have defended them, even by going to war if necessary. But now we will give them up. We are afraid that if we exercise our neutral rights we may sooner or later find ourselves in the embarrassing position of having either to back down or to fight." It was surely the tamest surrender of neutral rights, even before they were violated, ever staged by a great country.

In this ignoble position, with our heads in the sand, we remained for some time. Poland was destroyed, but for some eight months all was quiet on the western front. We congratulated ourselves. It was after all a "phony war." Then on May 10, 1940, Hitler struck, and within a few days Norway, Denmark, Holland, and Belgium (all of which, like the United States, hoped to get by without being involved) lost their political independence; within a few months France, for two hundred years the envied leader of European civilization, was a crushed and broken thing; and to everyone except the British it seemed that England would soon suffer the same fate. It was a great and unexpected shock for us. For the first time we began to realize that Hitler meant what he said. We began to understand a little that the Nazi philosophy and practice were a reversion to barbarism. For the first time we began to take note of the kind of world we were living in, and we found that it wasn't after all a world of normalcy.

The result was that we reversed our policy, although it took us some time, and even then we did not go the whole way. Having first abandoned neutrality by refusing to defend our neutral rights, we now abandoned it by giving unneutral aid to Great Britain. "Cash and carry" was replaced by "all aid short of war." All aid short of war was better than cash and carry, much better; but it revealed a state of mind scarcely less muddled. All aid short of war evidently meant, if it meant anything, that we regarded the preservation of the British Empire and the defeat of Hitler as being of vital importance to the United States. But we were still not ready to face the fact. By shouting "all aid" we could persuade ourselves that we were doing our utmost; but by whispering "short of war" we could persuade ourselves that the boys would not have to be sent overseas. We could give all aid without

41

giving the essential aid, and slip into the war without being in a "shooting war."

In this muddled state of mind we remained until Japan came to our aid by clarifying the issue. The attack on Pearl Harbor convinced us at last that some incredibly base and brutal force was loose in the world, that it was really our affair, and that all aid short of war wasn't good enough. We discovered, fortunately in time, what France and the small democratic countries of Europe discovered only when it was too late, that any country, as Somerset Maugham has said, which thinks more of its ease and comfort than of its freedom will lose its freedom, and the ironical thing about it is that it will lose its ease and comfort too.

4

Thus on various occasions the people of the United States tried to find ease and comfort by returning to normalcy. What did it get them? In domestic affairs it got them, after the Civil War, the Gilded Age of unsavory business enterprise and political corruption; and after the Wilson administration the era of Insull and the Great Depression. In foreign affairs it got them the Hawley-Smoot Tariff, the animosity of nearly every country in the world, twenty billion dollars in gold of no use to them or anyone else. It got them above all Pearl Harbor — got them involved in the very war which they had thought to avoid by returning to normalcy.

It is easy to see now the ineptitude of the policy of isolation which we followed after the last war. It is easy to see that if the United States had joined the League of Nations and had maintained a close alliance with Great Britain and France for preserving the peace of Europe the present war could have been avoided. Would this policy have been an "idealistic crusade to reform the world"? On the contrary, it would have been a most realistic and hard-headed way of serving our own interests. A similar policy on the part of Great Britain, France, and the lesser democracies of Europe would likewise have been realistic and hard-headed, and would likewise have served their interests. If this is "idealism," then by all means let us have more of it.

Both in domestic and in foreign affairs the horse-and-buggy days are gone, and in a world in which a man can travel from New York to India in less time than it took Benjamin Franklin to travel from Philadelphia to New York the attempt to escape into the Golden Age of normalcy is an invitation to chaos.

3

Can We Abate Nationalism and Curb the Sovereign State?

IN HUMAN AFFAIRS nothing is predetermined until after it has occurred. For this reason it is less futile to be concerned with the Golden Age of the future than with the Golden Age of the past. We cannot recover the past, but we can, within the limits set by nature and history and our own intelligence and resolution, make the future. We do make the future in any case. Even if, apathetic and resigned, we are content to let things ride; even if, afflicted with the impervious conservative mind, we strive in vain to return to the good old days — even so, we help to make the future. But in that case we make it by default; and since we help to make the future in any case, it is better to help make it, not by letting things ride, but by having some idea of where things ought to go and doing whatever is possible to make them go in that direction.

Fortunately, there are at all times a good number of people — intelligent, humane, liberal-minded people — who are more or less actively, more or less passionately concerned with the better world of tomorrow. They comprise the various brands of militant liberals, progressives, radicals, as distinguished from the various brands of conservatives and reactionaries.

They are, although they don't much like just now to be called so, "idealists" — people who are distressed or appalled by the injustice and suffering that is in the world, who are more or less profoundly convinced that the world can be shaped closer to the heart's desire, and who have more or less definite ideas of how it can be done. That is their merit, and a great merit it is. Their chief weakness is that, living too much in the ideal world of tomorrow, they are prone to forget or ignore how inert and toughly resistant the world of today really is; so that, as other men look back to a Golden Age that never existed, they too often look forward to a Golden Age that cannot in fact be created.

No one of course is ever exclusively concerned with either the past or the future. Everyone is always concerned with both at the same time, but for the most part only in respect to their private affairs. So far as public affairs are concerned, most of us, in humdrum times of peace, when everything is going on much as usual, are fairly content with the world as it is. We are not easily stirred by appeals to our better nature in matters that do not touch us personally, or much disposed to enlist in crusades for causes so remote as the better world of tomorrow. But in times of great disturbance, in times of war especially, when the ordinary routine of life is upset and our private lives and interests are threatened, we are easily persuaded that something is radically wrong with the world and that something, even if we don't quite know what, should be done about it. Then the latent idealism that is in all of us comes to the surface; and, generally speaking, the more unideal the world becomes, the more disposed we are to believe that an ideal world can be created.

Just now the world is about as far removed from the ideal, about as far sunk in barbarism and sheer brutality, as it has ever been. The consequence is that we realize as never before that something is radically wrong and that something must be done about it. We are under great pressure, as we were during the last war, to believe that it is not our fault, and that we are fighting only for the most unselfish reasons, for the highest, the ideal values — the Four Freedoms if you like. This is a quality of our virtues. Like President Roosevelt, we all "hate war." We hate the thing itself, however necessary it may be under the present particular circumstances. We know that war, especially under modern conditions, is a ghastly enterprise and that to win this war we must conduct it on its own terms of ruthlessness and brutality. This we cannot do effectively without believing that the enemy is solely responsible, or with a good conscience without believing that victory will more than compensate us for all the sacrifices we are making. We are therefore easily persuaded that when the war is over, the people of the United Nations, chastened by the harsh experience of the war, will be in a mood to work for a new and better world with the same zeal and unity of purpose which they now exhibit in defending themselves against the common danger.

This is a good frame of mind to be in, since nothing really good is likely to be accomplished unless we think rather better of ourselves than on the record of past achievements we perhaps deserve. But there is a danger in this frame of mind. The danger is that under the stress of war our thinking is apt to proceed with more heat than light; and in the ensuing fog complicated historical situations appear to be the result of simple causes, and complex social and international evils seem to be curable by simple remedies. In the last war the people of the Allied Nations were quite sure that the effective cause of the war was German "autocracy," symbolized by the Kaiser, and German "militarism," symbolized by the Prussian war lords. President Wilson's popularity and power came from the fact that he expressed this profound conviction in emotionally convincing terms. He persuaded the "plain people everywhere" that the single object of the war, so far as the Allied Nations were concerned, was to free the world, including Germany, from "the military masters of the German people." When this was done, so he said and so people thought, the peace-loving peoples of the world would gladly unite in a League of Nations to assure all peoples the right to govern themselves, to prevent future wars, and thereby make it safe for all countries to disarm.

It now seems incredible that so many people could have believed that so much could be accomplished all at once by such simple means. The price paid for having been led to expect too much on too easy terms was the disillusionment of the "lost generation" after 1919. It is highly desirable that we should not again pay that price for hopes set too high. There is less danger of it now than during the last war. We have probably learned something since 1919. We have rightly set our hopes on making a better world, but we are on the whole less sure that military victory in itself will provide us with an opportunity to do so, and we are more

47

aware that in any case the difficulties will be formidable. A multitude of books and pamphlets, and many statements by high officials in many countries, however, indicate that a great many people are now engaged in the same kind of wishful thinking that prevailed during the last war. To these people it seems obvious, as indeed it must be to everyone, that many of the evils of the modern world, including war as the chief evil, are somehow connected with those complex forces which we denote by the words "nationalism," "the sovereign state," "power politics," and "imperialism." It is equally obvious that the evils inherent in these complex forces are nowhere so flagrantly exhibited as in the countries with which we are now at war. To many intelligent, humane, and liberal-minded people the remedy seems equally obvious — nationalism must be abated, the power of the sovereign state must be curbed, power politics must be abandoned, imperialism must be ended; and for these things we must substitute a fraternal spirit of co-operation, and create another League of Nations or a Federation of States, supported this time by an "international police force" strong enough to suppress aggression by any one country against any other.

In the period before our Civil War it was said of the militant Abolitionists that they might be "wrong-headed," but that they were at least "wrong-headed in the right direction." The humane and liberal-minded international idealists of our time are, I think, expecting too much too soon; but their expectations are at least pointed in the right direction. In making a better world let us by all means look in that direction, and let us even expect much; but let us not expect the impossible. Admitting that evils have flourished and that crimes have been committed in the name of nationalism, the sovereign state, power politics, and imperialism, let us examine these complex forces a little in order to see whether they can, after all, be abruptly discarded; and if not, whether they should not be regarded, since we have to take account of them in making a better world, as relatively good or relatively bad according to the relatively good or relatively bad use that is made of them. And first of all, nationalism and the sovereign state.

1

What is a nation? It is not easy to define the term precisely. About all that one can say is that any fairly large group of people living in a particular country that regards itself as a nation is one. Such a group is more likely to regard itself as a nation if it has a common language, a common racial origin, common ideas about morality and religion, and a government of its own choosing. But none of these things, nor all of them together, will necessarily make a nation of any group of people. It is easier to recognize a nation than to say precisely what makes it one.

The inhabitants of Switzerland are certainly a nation — one of the smallest. Switzerland is about twice the size of the state of New Jersey and has about half as many inhabitants — an area of about sixteen thousand square miles, and a population of about four million. There is no Swiss language; in different regions German, French, and Italian are the languages of the people. There is no common religion; some of the people are Protestants, some Catholics. Yet in spite of these differences the people regard themselves neither as Germans, French, nor Italians, but as Swiss; and they form a nation because for centuries they have lived together under a government which they control and to which they are loyal, and have developed certain peculiarly Swiss customs, a certain "Swiss way of life," which they prefer to any other.

The fact that the Swiss have lived so long under a government of their own choosing has had much to do with making them a united nation. But living together under the same government for a long time does not in itself make a nation. Before 1914 about fifty million people were subject to the government of the Austro-Hungarian Monarchy. About one fourth of them were Austrian Germans, about one fourth were Hungarians, and about one half were Slavs; but the Slavs were of different sorts — Poles, Czechs, Slovaks, Ruthenians, Rumanians (not Slavic in origin, but essentially so in customs), Croats, Serbs, Slovenes. There were also a good number of Italians. There were at least as many languages as groups, and at least three religions — Roman Catholic, Protestant, and Greek Catholic. Before 1867 most of these groups had been ruled for a long time by the Austrian Habsburg emperors, but in 1867 the Constitution of the Dual Austro-Hungarian Monarchy gave to all of the groups the right to elect representatives to the assemblies that made the laws. Nevertheless, in 1914 Austro-Hungary was not a united nation, but a conglomeration of bitterly hostile nations, and it was the determination of the Slavic peoples to win their independence from a government largely controlled by the Germans and the Hungarians that precipitated the World War of 1914.

Still, there is nothing in the nature of Germans, Hungarians, Poles, Czechs, Slovaks, Rumanians, Serbs, Croats, Slovenes, and Italians to prevent them from living together in harmony as part of one nation and being loyal to its government. All of them have in fact come in considerable numbers to the United States, where they have soon lost their mutual antagonisms and have become good Americans and loyal subjects of a government which they had no share in creating and cannot control in their own interest. Why do all of these different people, who could not unite to form a nation in Austria-Hungary, so easily unite to form part of a nation in the United States?

The United States is certainly a nation — one of the largest and certainly one of the most united — and yet by all the tests of racial origin, language, religion, and inherited customs it should be neither united nor a nation. Here are one hundred and forty million people, spread out over an area of about three and a half million square miles. They are not descended from ancestors who have lived in the country from time out of mind, who have inherited and transmitted common racial qualities, a common language, and common ideas about morality, religion, and government. On the contrary, they are descended from ancestors who at some time within the last three centuries came to America from virtually every country in the world. Approximately twelve million of the one hundred and forty million were themselves born in some foreign country. The foreign-born Poles in the United States

would make a city larger than Warsaw (larger than
it was before Hitler destroyed it); the foreign-born
Italians would make a city larger than Rome. Probably more languages are used every day in the United
States by some group of citizens than in any other
country. As for religion, the only bond of unity is the
universal disposition to tolerate all religions. The
World Almanac lists more than a hundred distinct denominations (not counting the various forms within
some of the denominations, such as the Methodist),
ranging from the Roman Catholic Church, with about
twenty million members, to the Apostolic Overcom-
ing Holy Church of God with less than a thousand.

It was Goethe, I think, who said: "America, you
have it better." I once asked a Greek, the proprietor
of a candy and ice-cream shop who had been in the
United States about five years, how he liked it over
here. He had probably never heard of Goethe, but he
agreed with him. He said: "I like it fine. I am a Greek
Jew. So what? No one asks me am I a Greek Jew. I pay
the rent on time? Yes. So I am okay. My candy and
ice cream is good, high class. So the boys and girls
should worry I am a Greek Jew. I am here as good as
the next one. The children, they go to school. There
is nothing to pay. They read and speak American better than me. Already I am not understanding the
words they use. Already they are not Greeks any more,
but Americans. In America is better chance for all
poor people like me."

In general what makes these one hundred and forty
million people, gathered from the ends of the earth, a
nation is the profound conviction, on the part of native and foreign-born, that the U.S.A. is the place

where everything is better — the place in the world where life is easiest and men most free to do what they like and get what they want. "Land where our fathers died!" Well, yes, perhaps; but so many of our fathers, if we go back a few generations, died somewhere else. It is the U.S.A., rather than its rocks and rills and templed hills, that we love. We are attached to the country less for what it is than for what it has to offer. The Swiss love Switzerland for no such reason. They know well that in Switzerland life is not easier or men more free than in many other countries. They love Switzerland, not for what it has to offer everyone who comes, but for what it is to them. To them it is the homeland, the birthplace, the place where their fathers lived before them — the place which is beloved because it is so intimate and familiar, and so familiar because nothing changes much or rapidly from generation to generation, neither the people nor their farms and the villages nor the age-old customs of the country.

The influences which make any people a united nation are many and complex, and they vary from country to country. But whatever the influences may be, the resulting feeling of group kinship and attachment to a particular country is one of the chief characteristics of what we mean by the term "nationalism." In this sense nationalism is nothing new. In the sixteenth century, and long before that, Englishmen must have felt in some degree what only Shakespeare could express so well:

> This royal throne of kings, this sceptered isle . . .
> This other Eden, demi-paradise . . .
> This happy breed of men, this little world . . .
> This blessed plot, this earth, this realm, this England.

But nationalism as we know it in the modern world is something more than love of native land. In our time it has come to be identified with "patriotism," which is love of one's native land reinforced by unquestioning loyalty to the established government. It is this union of the feeling of group kinship, love of native land, and allegiance to the authority of the sovereign state that makes nationalism what it is today — the dominant political force in the modern world.

The idea of unquestioned allegiance to the sovereign territorial or national state is not strictly new. It was familiar to the ancient Greeks and Romans, but for many centuries it disappeared. The Romans gradually conquered virtually all the people living round the Mediterranean and created an empire which embraced virtually all that was then known to them as the civilized world. For some two centuries the Imperial government maintained peace and a reasonable degree of material prosperity, so that the sentiment of nationalism more or less disappeared. The consciousness that one was a Greek or a Persian or a Briton remained, but it was less important than the fact that one was a citizen of the Empire. The terms "Roman Empire" and "Roman law" came therefore to have a universal rather than a merely local and territorial significance. The term "Roman Empire" came to mean much the same thing as "civilization," because there was no known civilization outside of it; and the term "Roman law" came to mean much the same thing as "law of nature" or "law of reason," because it was the only law that prevailed in the civilized world. "The spirit of Rome," said the German jurist von Jhering,

54

"was an acid which, coming into contact with national-
ity, dissolved it."

In his famous history, *The Decline and Fall of the
Roman Empire,* Edward Gibbon says that the second
century "was the period in the history of the world,
in which the condition of the human race was most
prosperous and happy." In that time of peace and
prosperity many men cherished the idea that Rome
was "the eternal city," and that the Roman Empire
and the high civilization it maintained throughout the
known world would last forever. But in the third and
fourth centuries peace and prosperity disappeared,
and there began that slow and tragic "fall of the Roman Empire" which everyone has heard of, but the
causes of which no one has been able to determine with
certainty. By the year 800, at all events, the fall was
complete. In place of the one Roman Empire and the
one Greco-Roman civilization, there were many independent governments and three distinct types of
civilization — in eastern Europe the Greek Byzantine,
in Asia and Africa and Spain the Arab, in western Europe the medieval Christian; and the important point
is that what united the people within each of these regions and gave character to the civilization in each of
them, was not the sentiment of nationalism or loyalty
to the sovereign state, but attachment to different and
hostile forms of religion — in Arab-controlled countries Mohammedanism, in the Byzantine Empire the
Greek Catholic, and in western Europe the Roman
Catholic form of Christianity.

In western Europe after the fall of the Roman Empire there emerged a multitude of warring feudal

princes and kings maintaining a precarious control over territories of which the boundaries were not clearly defined and were always changing. In the "Dark Ages" of the ninth and tenth centuries the civilization of ancient Greece and Rome virtually disappeared. Latin ceased to be the spoken language and was replaced by local dialects — Romance or Germanic — which developed into the modern European languages. Political divisions, mixture of races, and divergent customs prepared the way for the formation of the various nations and national cultures of modern times. Yet even in the "Dark Ages" of the ninth and tenth centuries the rudiments of ancient learning were preserved and a certain unity of customs and ideas was maintained by the Roman Catholic Church, which imposed upon warring princes and divergent peoples a common religion and obedience to the Church and its officials, the pope and the bishops. It was largely through the unifying influence of the Roman Catholic Church and the Roman Catholic religion that western Europe emerged from the barbarism of the tenth century, and that, in spite of diversity in government, language, and custom, it formed one "Christian community" and produced the brilliant "medieval Christian" civilization of the twelfth and thirteenth centuries.

Throughout this long period of a thousand years neither the Roman idea of a supreme universal empire nor the modern idea of many sovereign independent states could be fully realized. The central political fact was the existence of two separate authorities, neither of which could command the loyalty and obedience of its subjects in all matters. Every man, in whatever country he might live — France, Germany, Italy, England — owed obedience and loyalty to the Church and its officials in "spiritual" matters; and to the Church he paid certain taxes and by its courts he was tried and punished for certain crimes and offenses. But at the same time he owed obedience and loyalty to the civil government of his own country in "temporal" matters; and to the overlord or king he paid certain other taxes, and by their courts he was tried and punished for certain other crimes and offenses. Between these two authorities, each demanding allegiance from the same people, conflict was sure to arise; and the history of western Europe in the Middle Ages is in no small part a history of the persistent conflict between Church and State — between the pope and the bishops who endeavored to maintain the authority of the Church throughout the Christian community, and the kings and princes who endeavored to acquire supreme authority within their own territories over all people, clergy as well as laymen, in respect to all matters, spiritual as well as temporal.

The outcome of this long struggle was the growing power of kings and the declining power of the pope, until the triumph of the State over the Church was assured by the Protestant revolution of the sixteenth century. The rise of Protestant religious ideas was the result of many causes, but no form of Protestant faith could survive in any country unless it was recognized and supported by the government of that country; so that in those countries that became Protestant, such as England, the new churches became state institutions completely subject to the state. The result was much the same in those countries, such as France and Spain, that remained Catholic, since in those countries the pope and bishops had to concede to the king, as the price paid for the suppression of heresy, many rights and privileges which they had formerly enjoyed. This transfer of power from Church to state was completed during the hundred years of civil and international "Wars of Religion" — a ruthless and uncompromising struggle for political power in which neither the Catholic nor any form of Protestant faith could survive in any country except by soliciting the aid, recognizing the authority, and submitting to the power of the government of that country.

Thus the united "Christian community" of western Europe disappeared. In place of one church and one religion there were many churches and many religions; and it was largely in defense of religious freedom that the great kings — Henry VIII, Francis I, Charles V, Philip II — became "absolute" rulers within their own countries, and that the sovereign independence of states became a fact. With the coming of the fact came the theory to support it. Machiavelli, in his famous book, *The Prince* (about 1513) defined the state as sheer political power, declared that the sole function of princes and rulers was to acquire and to use power, and that in using their power they were the sole judges of the ends to be attained by it, and need not be restrained by the rules of morality and religion that were binding upon private individuals. The successors of Machiavelli were on the whole less "Machiavellian" than Machiavelli himself. But Jean Bodin (*The Republic,* 1576), Hugo Grotius (*The Rights of War and Peace,* 1625), and many other political theorists of the seventeenth century, both law-

58

yers and bishops, defended the absolutism of kings and the sovereign independence of states on the basis of divine right, or the law of nature, or the common practice of states in present and past times. In the eighteenth century it was commonly taken for granted that the states of Europe, great and small, were independent of any higher authority, and that the government of each state could rightfully claim the unquestioned allegiance of all of its subjects, whether laymen or clergy, in respect to all matters, spiritual as well as temporal.

During the liberal-democratic revolution of the eighteenth and nineteenth centuries the form of government in the various European states was more or less radically changed. The absolutism of kings was abolished, and the power of government placed, in part or entirely, in the hands of assemblies of representatives elected by the people. But abolishing the absolutism of kings did nothing to weaken the absolutism of the state. On the contrary, the liberal-democratic revolution made the various states at once more secular and more independent. The will of the people instead of the divine right of kings was regarded as the source of sovereignty; and loyalty and obedience of citizens, formerly sanctioned by religion and enforced by the arbitrary will of the king, became more unqualified than ever because they were now thought of as loyalty freely rendered to the "nation" — loyalty to the people themselves, to the country they loved, and to the liberties they had won.

In the free-thinking, skeptical civilization of the modern world, in which all religions are tolerated and none can enforce the allegiance of any individual, in which all ideas are freely entertained and all opinions freely expressed, critical analysis has weakened or destroyed many of the preconceptions and beliefs which formerly provided the effective bonds of social union. But there remains, in all the historically created nation-states, one sentiment and one conviction which virtually all men share — the sentiment of nationalism, the conviction that it is the patriotic duty of every man to defend, with his life if necessary, the independence of the nation to which he belongs. As formerly men were willing to fight and die for church and religion, so the modern man is willing to fight and die for state and country.

2

Nationalism in any sense is always an important political force, but it is only as exhibited in what I have called the historically created nation-state that it reaches the level of a religious faith. By a historically created nation-state I mean one that has been created by a clearly defined nation, largely through its own efforts and as a result of a long period of continuous historical development. Not all historically created states are nation-states, nor are all nation-states historically created in this sense. The Austro-Hungarian Monarchy in 1914 was a historically created state — the result of a long and continuous historical development. It was not, however, a nation-state, but a collection of different and hostile nations whose bitter antagonisms weakened and finally destroyed it. Poland as of 1939 might be called a nation-state, but not, strictly speaking, historically created — not created by the Poles themselves through a long period of historical development. In the eighteenth century it was a loose union of feudal principalities, for a long time dominated and then partitioned by Russia, Austria, and Prussia. So it remained until the end of the last war, when it was restored by the victorious powers. But the restoration of Poland in the twentieth century, like its partition in the eighteenth, was an arrangement made by the great powers in their own interests. Much the same might be said of the Balkan states created in 1919. There are many nations in the Balkans, in Asia, Africa, and the East Indies, but they are not the centers of much, if any, political power because they have exhibited little or no capacity to construct states or governments through which the national sentiment can find political expression.

Since we are now fighting for the right of nations to govern themselves, it is natural to say, as the Atlantic Charter says, that all nations must be assured the right of living under governments of their own choosing. This sounds very well, but when we say it are we really thinking of the people of Burma or the tribes of North Africa? I suspect that we are thinking chiefly of the people who were living under governments of their own choosing when the war began. We are thinking chiefly of the clearly defined historically created nation-states. The ones that come most easily to mind are China, Japan, Russia, Turkey, Greece, Italy, Germany, Spain, Portugal, France, Switzerland, Holland, Belgium, Denmark, Norway, Sweden, Finland, Great Britain, the United States, Mexico, and the states of South America. In this list should certainly be included Canada, Australia, New Zealand, and South Africa. But although they are nations living under

61

governments of their own choosing, they are not technically independent states, but parts of the British Empire. Together with Great Britain they form the
British "Commonwealth of Nations," which might
well be taken as one of the historically created nation-
states — and one of the most powerful. At all events,
the historically created nation-states are the centers of
durable and effective political power in the modern
world. Some of them have great power, others much
less or very little. The extent of their power depends
on size, population, natural resources, industrial organization, and the like; but the thing that transforms
this material power, great or small, into political
power, that gives the state its character and makes it a
durable and resistant force in the world, is the sentiment of nationalism in the broad sense — the feeling
of the people that they are a nation distinct from other
nations, their love of native land and attachment to
the familiar customs of the country, and above all
their profound aversion to being governed or otherwise dominated, however efficiently, by any other nation or state.

All men have other obligations than those to the
nation-state and exhibit allegiance to other causes —
to local communtiy, to political party, to religion, to
science and the search for truth, to international peace
and the brotherhood of man. But the history of the last
two hundred years demonstrates well enough that for
the great majority of men all other obligations and al-
legiances, when brought into irreconcilable conflict
with allegiance to the nation-state and the obligation
to defend it, are defeated. Three outstanding exam-
ples will suffice to illustrate this point. The first is the

defeat of democratic internationalism during the French Revolution, the second is the defeat of international Socialism during the last war, and the third is the defeat of international Communism at the present time.

The intellectual movement of the eighteenth century known as the Enlightenment, which gave birth to the ideas of liberal democracy, was in spirit and in the logic of its ideas essentially international or cosmopolitan rather than national. The doctrine of natural rights implied that all men had the same rights, and that the form of government best suited to secure these rights would be the same for all nations. The French Revolution of 1789 was based upon this doctrine; and the most ardent defenders of the Revolution in the crucial years of 1792–3 came to regard the Revolution in France as merely the beginning of a world-wide revolution which would free the oppressed peoples everywhere from the tyranny of kings and the privileges of aristocrats. The Revolution, they said, is not merely a national but an international revolution: we are fighting for the freedom, not merely of the French people from the tyranny of the French king, but for the freedom of all peoples from the tyranny of all kings.

When the war with Austria broke out in 1792, this view was set forth in the official Declaration of Assistance and Fraternity to Foreign Peoples. "The National Convention declares, in the name of the French people, that it will accord fraternity and assistance to all peoples who shall wish to recover their liberty, and charges the generals . . . to furnish assistance to those peoples and to defend those citizens who may have been or who may be harassed for the cause of liberty." The Declaration was addressed more particularly to the people of Belgium, then governed by Austria, whose country the French armies were invading. Many of the Belgian people were French-speaking people and sympathized with the ideas of the French Revolution; but they, like all other Belgians, resented the presence of the French armies, and although they had been "harassed for the cause of liberty," they did not want to have liberty imposed on them by the French generals, especially when it required them to accept the depreciated French paper money. The ideas of liberal democracy spread from France to many countries; and Napoleon, conquering most of Europe, posed as a "liberator" and aimed to establish a "new order" which would give to the peoples of Europe the liberal institutions and freedoms which the Revolution had given to the French. But Napoleon was defeated, and what defeated him was the sentiment of nationalism — the aversion of the peoples of Europe to French intervention and control, and their preference for their own long-established governments, whether chosen by themselves or not.

In the nineteenth century Karl Marx formulated the doctrine of Socialism, or Communism as it is now called. This doctrine was also in its spirit and in the logic of its ideas international rather than national. The general idea was that the masses, the industrial workers especially, were exploited by the "capitalist" class in each country; that existing governments were controlled by the capitalist class for that purpose; and that conflicts and wars between countries were engineered by the capitalists and served the interests of the capitalist classes only. So far as the industrial workers were concerned, such conflicts and wars served only to keep them in subjection; so that by being "patriotic" they were merely being deluded and made to fight for interests that were not theirs. The real interest of the people — the "proletarians" — in every country was the same; and the struggle which should concern them was the international revolution, the struggle of all proletarians throughout the world to free themselves from all capitalist exploiting classes throughout the world. In closing his famous *Communis Manifesto* (1849) Karl Marx expressed this idea by saying: "Proletarians of all countries, unite! You have nothing to lose but your chains!"

In the early twentieth century there were in all European countries, except England, strong Socialist organizations of industrial workers, and strong Socialist political parties which included many who were not industrial workers. These parties accepted, with some "revision," the revolutionary international ideas of Marx. They regarded themselves as parts of an international Socialist organization which represented the common interests of the people in all countries as against the common interests of the capitalist ruling classes in all countries. They were, therefore, strongly anti-nationalist, anti-militarist, anti-imperialist; and they believed, sincerely enough, that if all the Socialist parties in Europe acted as a united party they could prevent a war by not being "patriotic" and by refusing to mobilize. On the eve of the war in 1914 there were many who believed the allegiance of the working classes to international Socialism would prove stronger than their allegiance to the governments of their respective countries, and that they would therefore be able to prevent the war. A meeting of representatives from the various Socialist parties was in fact assembled at Brussels with that end in view. But nothing came of it. For many reasons it was impossible for the Socialists in any country to refuse to mobilize. They knew that refusal to mobilize was equivalent to treason and might be punished as such. The Socialists in any country could not be sure that their brothers in other countries would stick it out. Socialist solidarity rested on the brittle foundation of abstract principles and reasoned conclusions rather than on habit and emotion; and when it came to the test, habit and emotion prevailed — the emotional allegiance of the workers to the nation was stronger than their allegiance to the Socialist international ideal.

No one has expressed this better than Jules Romains in *Death of a World* (Volume VII of *Men of Good Will*). Referring to the French workers and peasants in August 1914, he says:

It did not take them six days to persuade themselves that the bugles were blowing to the last great battle for Liberty, Justice, and Civilization. The voice of History, they decided, was summoning them to take part in the supreme struggle, begun a hundred and twenty years earlier, but again and again interrupted and postponed, of Democracy against Absolutism, to join in the marshalling of the Peoples against the Kings and the Emperors. The object to be attained was not so much the defeat of the Germans and the Austrians as the striking of the fetters from their limbs. Even . . . in the papers of the revolutionary Left . . . all references to imperialist guilt, to joint conspiracy of the capitalist governments, to the indifference which

good working-class men should show to the criminal call
of patriotism, were soon seen to be out of fashion. All
these over-recent cries of an academic ideology writhed
like strips of tinfoil in a furnace and vanished, touching
the flames with a faint and fugitive discoloration. No
longer was it a question of the class war, of Socialism, of
conflicting theories, but only of a Crusade, of the freeing
of the Holy Sepulchre.

During the last ten years we have watched international Communism suffer the same defeat in Russia.
After the war of 1914–18 Socialism recovered something of its former strength, and the most radical wing
of the Socialist parties, accepting the orthodox Marxian doctrine of violent revolution, took the name of
Communism. In Russia the war precipitated the Revolution of 1917, and the Revolution very soon came to
be controlled and directed by the radical Communist
or Bolshevist (majority) Party under the leadership
of Lenin and Trotsky. Both men regarded the Revolution in Russia as merely the beginning of an international revolution that would spread to all countries,
free the people from capitalist oppression, and establish "classless" societies in which the nationalist governments controlled by the capitalist classes would
"wither away." Lenin did not believe that the revolution could succeed in the long run in one country only;
and in his time the policy of the Soviet government
was designed to promote the cause of international
Communism by assisting and directing, through the
Third International (the Comintern), the Communist Parties in other countries. In those days, accordingly, a good Communist was expected to divest himself of all national prejudices. To be "patriotic," to

love "Mother Russia," was to be guilty of "bourgeois" sentimentalism. The first duty of the good Communist was to renounce his allegiance to the nation, to regard himself as a member of an international brotherhood, and to be loyal to the supreme cause of the international proletarian revolution.

But Lenin died in 1924, and in 1928 Joseph Stalin was able to expel Trotsky from the party and gain control of the government. From that time the policy of promoting the international Communist revolution was gradually abandoned. One reason for that was the course of events in other countries, especially the rise of Fascism in Italy and Germany, which made it clear that there was no possibility of a Communist revolution in any other country within any reasonable time. Partly for this reason Stalin believed that the main task was to establish Communism in Russia, and he realized that in order to do so it was necessary to win the support of the Russian people. Not more than two million Russians were members of the Communist Party. The great majority of the Russian people were but little interested in Communist theory, and cared nothing at all about promoting a world-wide Communist revolution. What they wanted was a government that would make things better for them and for Russia. No people in the world has a greater attachment to native land than the Russians. Their love of "Mother Russia" could not be destroyed by official decree or any amount of intellectual indoctrination; and by far the best way to win their loyal support of the Soviet government was to appeal to their love of country — to make them feel that accepting Communism, being loyal to the Soviet government, and loving

"Mother Russia" were but different aspects of one supreme and undivided allegiance.

For these reasons Stalin subordinated the cause of international Communism to the national interests of Russia. He continued, through the Third International (Comintern), to tell the Communists in other countries what they should think and do with every shift in the international situation; but his foreign policy was designed primarily to promote and defend the national interest. He let it be known that one could now be a good Communist and still love "Mother Russia." Famous "bourgeois" writers, such as Gogol and Tolstoy, could now be praised by the critics because they were so essentially Russian, and because their writings exhibited both the virtues and the defects of the Russian character with so much sympathetic understanding. Russian history ceased to be taught purely from the Communist point of view; and the great czars, such as Ivan the Terrible and Peter the Great, ruthless oppressors of the people though they were, could now be admired because they contributed so much to the creation of the Russian nation.

This shift from the international to the national policy was bitterly resented by Trotsky and the old Bolsheviks who had been associated with Lenin in carrying through the Revolution. "The Revolution has been betrayed," they said — betrayed by Stalin. But the Revolution had not been so much betrayed by Stalin as defeated by circumstances. Communism could be firmly established in Russia only by winning the support of the Russian people, and to win the support of the Russian people it had to make terms with Russian nationalism. Allegiance to international Communism was thus defeated by the far stronger allegiance to Mother Russia. Nothing was needed to make the defeat complete and final but the invasion of Russia by the German army. The Soviet government, in defense of the national interest, had to make an alliance with all the anti-Communist, "bourgeois" governments that were fighting Hitler. As a concession to them the Comintern had to be abolished; and the British and American people can now admire the Soviet government because the heroic resistance of the Russian people is inspired, not by the determination to defend their government because it is Communist, but because it is Russian.

3

The sentiment of nationalism in this broad sense is the principal political force of our time; and the historically created nation-state is the form which political power takes in the modern world. Whether the political power of any state is great or little depends upon the size of the country, its population, the material resources available, and the capacity of the people for effective industrial organization and political activity. According to international law, all states recognized as sovereign and independent are equal in rights; but the actual power with which such states can defend and promote these rights varies enormously, ranging all the way from the very slight power of such states as Thailand or Switzerland to the very great power of such states as the United States, Russia, or the British Empire. That political power exists in this form and will be used by each state, whether great or small, to defend the rights and interests of the people, or what the people regard as their rights and interests, is a fact that must be accepted; and it is futile to base any plans for a new and better world in the immediate future on the assumption that the sentiment of nationalism will be replaced by the love of mankind, or that political power as now organized in sovereign independent states can be transferred, by pledges signed or treaties agreed upon, to a European or world federation of states.

To Lord Acton is attributed the statement: "Power corrupts and absolute power corrupts absolutely." That may or may not be true; but one thing is certainly true: we can never be sure that political power, whatever form it takes or whoever has it, will always be used with wisdom and restraint. Where political power is, there danger lurks, and the greater the power, other things being equal, the greater the danger. The small states are compelled to use their power, if not with wisdom, at least with more or less restraint because they have so little of it. It is the great states that are always open to the temptation to use their power without restraint — without due regard, or even without any regard, to the rights of states less powerful than themselves.

The great states have only too often used their power in this way — to take what they wanted because they wanted it and had the power to take it with impunity. There is no great country, so far as I know, that has not at some time or other despoiled some weaker neighbor with no better justification than the doctrine of Thrasymachus that "might makes right, justice is the right of the stronger." On no other ground can one justify the aggressive wars of Louis

XIV or Napoleon. The British cannot read with any pride the story of the conquest of Ireland in the seventeenth century, or of the Boer Republic in the twentieth. There is nothing to be said for our own war against Mexico in 1846 except that it was the "Manifest Destiny" of the United States to possess New Mexico and California — an argument that would permit any state to take its neighbor's territory if it had the power to do so. There is nothing to be said for our war against Spain in 1898 except that the Cubans were fighting for liberty, which was true but not the real reason for our coming to their aid. There is nothing to be said for our taking the Philippines except what President McKinley said, that it was our duty to "Christianize and civilize" the Filipinos, which we proceeded to do by a ruthless suppression of rebellion inspired by their desire to live under a government of their own choosing. In past and present times many offenses and even crimes have been committed in the name of "national interest," or "national honor," or the right of the sovereign state to maintain and increase its power by any means it might think necessary.

It is when we recall the long list of such offenses and crimes of aggression and spoliation, committed by the great states against weaker neighbors or against the "backward countries" of Asia and Africa, that we feel inclined to agree with the liberal and humane international idealists who say that " nationalism must be abated," the power of the sovereign state "must be curbed." And when, as so often happens, the people support such wars of aggression by crying "my country, right or wrong," we are apt to agree with the plethoric Dr. Johnson that "patriotism is the last refuge of a scoundrel." So it may be, and so it often has been. And if the scoundrel happens to be a complete egocentric like Napoleon, or a manic-depressive like Hitler, with command of a great country such as France or Germany, the crimes committed in the name of nationalism and the sovereign state may reach the point where that particular manifestation of nationalism and the sovereign state must indeed be abated and curbed — abated and curbed in the only way they can be, by opposing to them a force greater than their own.

This has often happened before, and now it has happened again. The crimes committed by Hitler go beyond anything recorded since the fanatical civil and international wars of religion in the sixteenth century. He has committed or authorized crimes against small nations in violation of all accepted rules of international law and of promises solemnly made and recorded. He has committed or authorized crimes against individuals, and particular groups of individuals, in violation of all established legal rights, of all religious teaching and every principle of morality and justice, and in ignorance or disdain of the most elementary sense of truth and decency and humane dealing. And all of these crimes have been frankly and cynically justified on the ground of nationalism, on the ground that the Germans are a "master race" and as such are under no obligation to respect the rights of inferior nations, and above all on the ground that "might makes right," that "equity is where the strength is."

Admitting that crimes have been committed in the name of nationalism and the sovereign state, and that no great state is guiltless, it is a sound instinct that

leads men to judge of crimes according to the purpose
that inspires them and the magnitude of their results.
So judged, the crimes committed by Hitler have been
sufficiently great to arouse first the loathing, then the
fear, and finally the united resistance of the greater
part of the world. We are at last all convinced that this
particular manifestation of nationalism and the power
of the sovereign state must be not only abated and
curbed, but destroyed; and the principal object of the
United Nations in this war is to destroy it. That it will
be destroyed is now certain. But if there is any one
thing more than another that has enabled so many nations to unite for that purpose and given them the will
and power to carry it through, it is precisely the sentiment of national patriotism and the determination of
men to defend at all costs the sovereign independence
of the state. Let us not, then, condemn as in itself evil
the very thing that in this time of crisis is saving us
and our "way of life" from destruction, or be deluded
by the notion that after the war is over we can abate as
a political force a sentiment which the war itself has
raised to the level of a religious faith.

After the war is over, nationalism, whatever its defects, will remain for any foreseeable future what it
has been for a long time past — the strongest political
force in the modern world; and this force will be exerted in the form of many sovereign independent
states. The sentiment cannot be abated or the power
curbed except in the sense that the people of any country can, if they have sufficient intelligence and moral
sense, use the power for purposes more enlightened
and ends more desirable because they take into account
the rights and interests of other nations.

4

Can We Abolish Power Politics and End Imperialism?

FOR GOOD or evil, words often have great influence in their own right, apart from the things they represent. Like actors on the stage, they have their entrances and their exits, play an important role for a time, and then lose favor. They may, like men, be born free and equal, but like men they have their ups and downs. Certain words in particular suddenly acquire greater prestige than they deserve, and then after a time, from too much use or because the things they refer to have become sinister or merely ridiculous, they lose their popularity and either cease to be used at all or are used only to distort what they originally represented.

Such a word is "creative," which for a long time played a minor and becoming role. Then one day some critic or other used it to boost a book that he happened to like. Mr. X, he announced, was a "creative writer." The word caught on, and now nothing is any good unless it is "creative." Writer, artist, critic, interior decorator, cook — if he be not "creative" he may as well be damned. Too much use has beaten all sense out of the word, so that it has become merely ridiculous. Another such word is "refined." In the nineteenth century a person of cultivation, good manners,

and good taste was a "person of refinement." It was a
compliment — as much as to say: "he is the genuine
article, a real guy." But in the course of time much of
what in the nineteenth century was regarded as good
manners and good taste came to seem artificial and
affected — something, like the Sunday suit, put on to
make one look slicker than one usually is; so that now
it is practically an insult to call a person "very refined." It means a person too nice and squeamish and
innocent to be let out alone nights. In respect to persons, the word now merely distorts the thing it originally represented, and can be used seriously only in
regard to products like sugar or alcohol.

Something of the same sort has happened to such
good old words as "politics," "power," "empire," and
"imperial." The term "politics" has taken on a certain
unsavory meaning, as when we say "playing politics,"
or "it's only politics." In international relations playing politics, otherwise known as "the diplomatic
game," has recently become a little more unsavory, or
even sinister, by being described as "power politics."
In the second century the term "Roman Empire"
meant much the same thing as the term "civilization";
and to speak of the "sway of Imperial Rome" was to
confer the highest distinction on that city. Long after
the Roman Empire disappeared the thing itself was
so much prized that men longed to have it restored,
and even added to its high prestige by calling it the
"Holy Roman Empire." But for a long time now the
terms "empire" and "imperialism" have been terms
of reproach.

During recent years the terms "power politics" and
"imperialism" have come to be more than terms of re-

proach; they have come to denote something wholly evil. The reason is that we identify them with the philosophy and practice of Hitler and the rulers of Japan. We are all convinced, and rightly so, that the kind of power politics which they practice and approve of is wholly evil, and that the kind of imperial domination which they aim to achieve is no less evil. And so all power politics and all imperialism seem to us wholly evil — something which we are not guilty of, something which we are fighting to destroy. It is chiefly for this reason that many people find it possible to think and say that after the war is over "power politics must be abandoned," that "imperialism must end," and that "the white man must get out of the Far East."

It will be worth while to trace the history of these terms, and to examine the things which they refer to, in order to see whether the things referred to are in themselves wholly evil and whether in any case they can be easily ignored or got rid of.

1

Something more than two thousand years ago the famous Greek philosopher Aristotle wrote a book, or left notes which were made into a book, entitled *Politics*. For Aristotle, and for the Greeks and Romans and the people of the Middle Ages, the term "politics" referred to the institutions, laws, customs, and moral and religious ideas by which men managed to live together in a community. Its meaning was not limited to the form of government and the making of laws, but included the economic activities and moral ideas of the community as well. But in the sixteenth century

77

Machiavelli discussed the art of government without reference to morality and ethics; and in the next two centuries certain writers dealt with the activities by which men make a living and acquire wealth as a separate subject, which was called "political economy" or "economics." Since that time the term "politics" has been commonly understood to refer to the form of government and laws and activities by which the people are governed. .

In the eighteenth century, when people were mostly governed by absolute kings, there were of course no elections and no political parties; but there were influential noble families, and industrial "guilds," and financial corporations — all representing certain interests, and all seeking to get the favor of the king. The head of a powerful noble family, for example, might for various reasons have great influence with the king (or with the king's minister, or the king's mistress), which of course he would use for getting what he wanted for his family or his friends. When he did this he was "playing politics," but that isn't what it was called at that time. It was said that he "had the ear of the king," or that he was "making use of his interest through the minister."

Then kings mostly lost their power, and in the nineteenth century in most European countries laws were made, as they are in the United States, by assemblies composed of representatives elected by the people. For getting the representatives elected and for advocating certain measures, political parties were formed; and those who made a business of managing the parties or getting elected to office were called "politicians." The term "politics" came then to have a double meaning. In general it referred to the form of government and the making of laws; but it also referred to the activities of politicians in winning elections and getting laws passed that would be agreeable to the people who supported their candidates. In an ideal democracy people are supposed to forget about their personal and private interests and to support measures that will serve the common interests of the nation. Many people do this all of the time, and most people do it some of the time. But it is not always, or often, easy to know what the common interest is, whereas it is always easy to know what is for the immediate interest of the individual or the group to which he belongs. In the United States there are many such groups — farmers, laborers, big business, commerce, the South, the industrial Northeast, the Middle West, and so on. It is no longer great families but these groups and sections that have a powerful "interest." They have not "the ear of the king," but they have the ear of their representatives in the House and Senate, and through them they have great influence in getting the laws passed that will be, or that they think will be, beneficial for them. They exert great "pressure," and this competitive struggle of the groups and sections for getting what they want whether it is for the common good or not is called "pressure politics." Since the groups have political power, it would be equally correct to call it "power politics."

The term "pressure politics" doesn't sound quite so bad as "power politics," and that may be why the one term is used for domestic politics whereas the other is reserved for international politics. But still, to those who are thinking of some ideal democracy, even the term "pressure politics" doesn't sound any too good. However it sounds, we all know that it expresses the way in which democracy actually works, and after all it is inevitable that it should work that way. By and large, men pursue their own interests, and where the interest of a group is clearly discernible and can be promoted or injured by legislation, it is inevitable that the group should try to promote or protect it by legislation. The practical justification for doing so is that democratic government rests on the will of the people, and the will of the people can be determined only by majority vote; and in practice the majority vote is determined by the competitive pressure of the various groups. The groups that at any time get what they want, by pressure on congressmen, log-rolling bargains, or otherwise, may be said to represent for that purpose and that time the will of the nation.

The trouble with this is that all people have many interests, some of which can be promoted by certain laws only at the expense of the others. Farmers and laborers are both "producers" and "consumers." As producers they want higher prices for what they sell; but as consumers they want lower prices for what they buy. Their interest as producers is more apparent to them, and more easily promoted by legislation, than their interest as consumers. Besides, everybody is a consumer and all consumers have, as consumers, the same interest; but the class of "everybody" which makes up the consumers is not organized, and therefore cannot easily exert "pressure" on legislation. We feel, therefore, that the term "pressure politics" doesn't sound quite right because pressure politics benefits only those who are organized to promote their private interests at the expense of the others. In such an emergency as the present war the term sounds worse than in times of peace. It is perfectly obvious that "playing politics" and "pressure politics" promote the private interest of some but interfere with the interest of the nation as a whole, which is to win the war and not to raise prices for farmers, or increase wages for industrial laborers, or secure fat profits for war contractors. We see this, and so with one accord, or almost with one accord, we say: "Playing politics and pressure politics are out for the duration." We do not say that pressure politics "must be abandoned after the war is over." We are not quite so naïve or befuddled as to believe that. We just say that it must be out for the duration. And even that is a little naïve, because obviously it isn't entirely out even for the duration.

The technique of politics in international affairs is much the same as in national affairs, but this fact is obscured because the conditions are somewhat different and we use different terms to describe it. We speak of "international relations" instead of international "politics," of "playing the diplomatic game" instead of "playing politics," of "power politics" instead of "pressure politics." In international politics the interests involved are independent states instead of groups or sections within the state; the interests are promoted by exerting "power" rather than "pressure"; and the conflict of interests is resolved, not by a legislative body enacting laws that can be enforced by judicial process, but by treaties or agreements voluntarily subscribed to by the states involved. If the interests are regarded as vital and cannot be reconciled by agreement, the only way out in international politics is war. In national politics the conflict of interests between groups or sections may also become irreconcilable by peaceful means, although in strongly united nation-states this is less likely to happen; but when it does happen, the way out is the same as in international politics — civil war, which is sometimes called revolution.

There is, however, one very important difference between national and international politics. The conditions which separate nations are ordinarily more deep-seated and permanent than those which separate groups within the nation. An English-speaking farmer in Iowa is, after all, not a "foreigner" to an English-speaking (or even a German-speaking) laborer in Detroit in the same sense, or to the same degree, that an Italian in Rome is a foreigner to an Englishman in London. For this reason the common interests of the various groups in the United States are more apparent, even if in the long run they are not more real, than the common interests of the various nations of Europe or of the world. And therefore the conflicts of interest more easily appear to be, even if they are not in fact, irreconcilable by peaceful means. And since there is no international government by which agreements can be enforced, any state which has sufficient power is in a position to use its power without any restraint except that which is self-imposed — the restraint which is imposed by its own sense of decency and justice. When the rulers of a powerful state, unrestrained by any sense of decency or justice because they have none, frankly adopt the doctrine that might makes right and ruthlessly act upon it, then "power politics" becomes the entirely evil thing that the present German government has made of it. But to suppose that power politics is always wholly evil because Hitler and his humorless, bleak-faced Nazi supporters have made a wholly evil use of it is only to obscure and distort the political realities of the world in which we live.

It obscures and distorts the political realities at the present moment by leading us to suppose that the United States is not, never has been, and never will be engaged in the game of "power politics" or concerned in anything so futile as the attempt to maintain peace by adjusting the "balance of power." The effect that can be produced by a slight shift in the use of words is indeed astonishing. We call attention every day to our great political power, to our mounting naval and military power, and to the certainty that this power will be sufficient to crush the power of Germany and Japan. Yet no one will admit that we are engaged in the nefarious business of power politics or that we are fighting for a restoration of the old balance of power. These are words that we associate with Germany and Japan. The things they represent must therefore be wholly evil. And so we easily delude ourselves by the notion that when Germany and Japan are crushed by our superior power, power politics will be abandoned and no one will be concerned to maintain a balance of power.

But if we regard things instead of words, it is clear that the term "power politics" is what the grammarians call a "redundancy." The simple fact is that politics is inseparable from power. States and governments exist to exert power, for the maintenance of order, the administration of justice, the defense of the community against aggression — in theory always and solely for these good ends. But the power, much or little, is always there, and will be used for some end, good, bad, or indifferent. In any country the government may be strong or weak. In the world at large there are great powers and minor powers. In each country and in the world at large there is either a stable balance of power, an unstable balance of power, or no balance of power at all. But there is always power. "Power," as Lionel Gerber says in his book *Peace by Power*, "never vanishes. If you do not wish to retain or wield it, somebody else will. You may feel the effects of power as a passive recipient; you may deal with it as an active agent. There is no escape, no immunity." Political power exists in the world and will be used by those who have it — for good ends we hope, but at all events for some ends.

In this very real sense all politics is power politics, and every accession of power redresses the balance in somebody's favor or to somebody's loss. The fact stands out before our eyes, grim and inescapable, as the controlling fact of our time — the fact that the present war is a manifestation of power politics on the grandest scale ever seen, and that the primary purpose of the United Nations in this game of power politics is to redress the balance of power against Germany and Japan and in their own favor. It will be said that the United Nations desire power only for good ends, whereas Germany and Japan desire it for bad ends. That is of course admitted. We cannot help thinking that the ends pursued by Germany and Japan are bad ends. Put at the lowest level, if you call it the lowest, they are bad ends because in so far as Germany and Japan gain power we lose it. That is enough to go on

84

with. But whatever good ends we intend to use our power for after the war is over, our capacity to realize those ends will not be improved by supposing that we are not fighting this war to acquire political power, or that the result of winning it will not be a balance of power that is favorable to us, or that we can maintain peace and order in the world without resorting to power politics — that is to say, without using the political power we have acquired.

After the war is over, there will still be power politics, and no doubt there will be evils connected with it; but it need not be, and we have good reason to suppose that it will not be, the wholly evil thing it has been in the hands of Germany and Japan. There will also be a balance of power, but that does not mean that we must or should return to the old balance-of-power *policy*. Hitler has indeed demonstrated, as Napoleon did before him, that the balance of power is not, like an electric clock, a self-regulating mechanism which needs only to be set up in order to keep the peace without further attention. That happy idea was born in the eighteenth century when there were, in Europe, six great powers about equally strong. The idea was that if each great power looked after its own interests without any regard to the others, any threatened domination by any one or two of them would automatically give rise to counteralliances sufficiently strong to redress the balance. Except for the smashing conquests of Napoleon, this idea worked well enough for two centuries, if not to prevent wars, at least to prevent any one power from destroying the political independence of any of the others. But this idea of a self-regulating balance will no longer serve any good purpose. The experience of the present war has shown that if each country looks after its own interests without regard to the others, the result is likely to be, not a stable balance of power, but a balance wholly in favor of aggressor states, and totally disastrous to the political and cultural independence of the others.

If peace is to be maintained by a proper balance of power, the balance must be in favor of those countries that desire to maintain peace and have the power to do so. It is after all Hitler and Hirohito who wish to destroy the balance of power, so that only the national interests of Germany and Japan can be served. When they are defeated the dominant power will be in the hands of Russia, Great Britain, the United States, and China, in so far as China can make politically effective the potential strength of her people and resources. We cannot get rid of the power at the command of these countries, or of the balance of power that will exist throughout the world as a consequence of their having it. We can only hope, and do what we can to make it come true, that each of these great states will be disposed to regard the balance of power, not as something to be upset on every favorable opportunity for advancing its own selfish interests, but rather as something to be adjusted by mutual agreement, and with constant and considered attention to the maintenance of peace and the promotion of prosperous intercourse among nations.

Even those who deplore great political power because it is inherently dangerous (or most of them — there are always Gandhi and his followers) recognize that a "new and better world" cannot be made without it. They say, and everybody says, that there can be no new and better world unless Great Britain, Russia, and the United States take a leading part in making it. But why these countries especially? Precisely because they have very great political power, precisely because they have sufficient power, if they work together, to determine what shall and shall not be done in the world and to see that it is or is not done. It is for this reason that these great states are so urgently recommended to assume their share of "the white man's burden" of "affording all nations the means of dwelling in safety within their own boundaries." They must, then, presumably, assume their share of this burden in the Far East as well as elsewhere. Nevertheless, many of the people who insist that they must take a leading part in doing all this are the very people who say that "the white man must get out of the Far East" and "imperialism must be ended."

This brings us to the question, what is imperialism and what are the imperialist countries?

2

The terms "empire," "imperial," "imperialism" have had different meanings at different times. But the political reality which gave birth to these terms is, and always has been, only the most obvious and spectacular manifestation of power politics — that is to say, of political power. At successive periods during the last four or five thousand years certain favorably placed peoples have, within the limits set by circumstances and their own capacity, extended their political power over peoples of diverse origin and culture. Such extensions of political power, whether continental or maritime, have been called empires; so that by common usage we speak of the Babylonian, the Assyrian, the Median, and the Persian empires of very ancient times; of the Athenian, the Alexandrian, the Roman empires of a somewhat later time; of the Moslem, the Mongol, the Venetian, and the German empires of medieval times; and of the Portuguese, the Spanish, the Dutch, the French, the British, the Russian, and the Chinese empires of modern times. We do not commonly speak of the United States empire. Why not? I do not know. Since the United States has acquired Alaska, Puerto Rico, the Hawaiian Islands and the Philippines, and has thereby acquired what Walter Lippmann calls political "commitments" extending over half the globe, it has, by every common test, the right to be recognized as an empire, as one of the great imperial powers.

In modern times the term ".empire" has come to be associated more particularly with those empires that have been created by what is called "colonial expansion." In the sixteenth and seventeenth centuries Spain, France, Holland, and England explored and colonized the new world of America; and Portugal, Holland, France, and England obtained certain possessions and trade rights in India and the East Indian islands. In the eighteenth century "colonial expansion" took the form of a conflict between England and France for the possession of India and North America, which resulted in the defeat of France, both in America and in India. After the Napoleonic Wars the colonial movement eased off a good deal; but during the last quarter of the nineteenth century there occurred a rapid and extensive expansion of European political and economic power in the so-called " backward countries" of the world. The continent of Africa was largely taken over by Great Britain, France, Belgium, Germany, and Portugal. Russia extended her political control over Siberia and central Asia. The United States acquired Alaska, Puerto Rico, the Hawaiian and the Philippine islands; and China was "opened up" — that is to say, the United States, Great Britain, France, Germany, and Russia acquired certain "extraterritorial" rights in China, such as the right to develop the economic resources of certain regions, the right to use certain ports as naval bases, and a variety of special rights in certain seaports known as "treaty ports." The opening up of China resulted in the Boxer Rebellion against the "foreign devils," but the armies of the foreign devils put down the rebellion, and then the Chinese government was required to pay heavy indemnities and to make certain further "concessions."

The reasons for this rapid expansion into "backward countries" were chiefly economic — the pressure of European and American business enterprise seeking new opportunities for profit, the great demand for certain commodities essential to modern industry, such as oil and rubber, the pressure for new markets for the manufactured goods of the industrialized countries, the demand for political intervention in order to recover loans made through European banks to native rulers who defaulted, and so on. Taken as a whole, it was a pretty sordid and unheroic business. No country that took part in it has much if anything to be proud of. The story of the Boer War, of the Spanish-American War, of the Russo-Japanese War, of the Boxer Rebellion, of the methods employed by the United States to prevent the Filipinos from living under a government of their own choosing — the story of any or all of these episodes is for the most part a story of the oppression of the politically weak for the economic advantage of the strong.

It is to this late nineteenth-century mercenary scramble for "backward countries" that the term "imperialism" now especially refers. The term has a bad smell, because the thing itself had a bad smell. The thing has a worse smell now because the reasons often given at the time for rather shady enterprises now sound purely hypocritical. President McKinley said that after the defeat of Spain he could not decide whether to take the Philippines. He asked for divine guidance, and then suddenly, he knew not why, it was clear to him. To restore the Philippines to Spain would be "dishonorable"; to allow them to fall into the hands of Germany or Japan would be "bad business"; to recognize their independence would mean misrule and anarchy. He therefore decided that it was the duty of the United States to take the Philippines, "educate the Filipinos, and uplift and civilize and Christianize them as our fellow-men." The English writer Rudyard Kipling justified the imperialism of the time in the same way, although he was far less crude, far more "refined," in his way of doing so than President McKinley. He invented the term "White Man's Burden," which became famous and has now acquired a merely cynical or hypocritical sound.

> Take up the White Man's burden —
> Send forth the best ye breed —
> Go bind your sons to exile
> To serve your captives' need;

> To wait, in heavy harness,
> On fluttered folk and wild —
> Your new-caught, sullen peoples,
> Half-devil and half-child.

The idea was that if the white man took over the backward countries and ruled the backward peoples, it was for their own good: the little profit to be derived was no more than a fair return for bringing them the blessings of Western, Christian civilization.

This is but a recent version of the idea which has always been used to justify European conquest of other countries and alien people. Vasco da Gama, upon landing in India in the sixteenth century, is reported to have said: "We come in search of Christians — and spices:" And to Columbus is attributed the saying: "Gold is excellent; gold is treasure, and he who possesses it does all that he wishes to in this world, and succeeds in helping souls into paradise." Neither man could perceive the irony that for us invests these statements with a cynical meaning not intended. They really believed that it was the "white man's burden" to Christianize and civilize the benighted races of the world, but we can no longer pronounce the phrase with a straight face. Since the time of Columbus, even since the time of Kipling, we have learned all about the subconscious, and how it enables us to conceal the "real" reasons for what we do by offering the "good" reasons which will sustain our moral credit. This is all very well. But, as often happens with a new idea, we have overdone it. In our reversion from the naïve self-deception of an earlier age we have gone too far and are in danger of becoming wise guys who deceive themselves by supposing that the real motives are always sordid and the professed motives never sincere.

Thus the term "imperialism" has fallen into complete disrepute. It refers only to the evils that have been associated with the colonial expansion of European states in Africa and Asia. To be an imperialist it seems that one must be a white man and a European, and a hidebound conservative, in national politics bent only on preserving class privilege, and in international politics inspired by nothing more laudable than the determination to hang on to the ill-gotten spoils of conquest in Asia and Africa. It is more or less to be taken for granted that an imperialist is either stupid or hypocritical, either a fool or a knave.

This doesn't matter much. What matters is that of all the great imperial countries the only one which our militant liberal internationalists seem to regard as imperialistic is Great Britain. From what I read I gather that neither the United States, Russia, nor China is now imperialistic; if they ever were, they have been converted. But Great Britain is still unregenerate, or its ruling class is; and it is the British Empire that will be the chief obstacle to a new and better world after the war is over. Our militant liberal internationalists are therefore much concerned for the salvation of the British Empire, and every week they pray for Mr. Churchill.

I open a recently published book on post-war reconstruction and find the following:

What broadly ought to be done with colonies in a world committed to abiding peace? Since colonies are the preserves of particular states no effective plan can be carried out unless the leading colonial powers cooperate by respectively undertaking measures that are necessary or desirable. *It so happens, however, that of the four greater powers among the allies three — the United States, Russia, and China — are virtually free from vested colonial interests. It may not be too visionary to hope that these could persuade the fourth, Britain, to join with them in setting up an entirely new regime in order to abolish the major evils and enmities that spring from colonial imperialism.*

This is a good example of a certain type of thinking about post-war reconstruction — thinking in terms of phrases or words with fixed meanings that distort the political realities. I suppose that if Siberia, with its eight or ten million of non-Russian inhabitants — Siberians, Chinese, Koreans — were an island or a group of islands separated from Russia by two thousand miles of water, there would be no difficulty in recognizing that Russia is an empire with very considerable "vested colonial interests." Or maybe the Chinese Empire would be regarded as imperialistic if Mongolia, Manchuria, Tibet, and Sinkiang were scattered about in the Indian Ocean and the southwest Pacific. Fortunately for us, the Middle West, and the Louisiana Territory acquired in 1802, are not separated from the Atlantic seaboard and from each other by large bodies of water, or we might suffer the disadvantage of being called the United Commonwealth of Nations and the American Empire. Apparently the best way for any people to avoid the stigma of imperialism is to be very prolific, running if possible to two hundred million, and to inhabit a great continent rather than a small island. It is at all events, I should think, not too visionary to suppose that if the United States, Russia, and

China tried to persuade Great Britain to set up an entirely new regime in respect to her colonial possessions, Great Britain would probably want to know whether it was intended that the new regime should apply to Siberia, Sinkiang, Tibet, Puerto Rico, Hawaii, and the Philippines. The causes of modern imperialism are fundamentally economic, and the remedy, which I shall discuss briefly in the final chapter, calls for something more than a friendly effort on the part of untainted governments to persuade the guilty to mend their ways.

The most unfortunate result of this distortion of the political realities is that it impairs the cordial relations which, both for winning the war and for making a durable peace, should exist between the United States and Great Britain. We have on all accounts more in common with the people of Great Britain and the British self-governing dominions than with any other people. We are united to them by a common language, a common literature, a common heritage of political ideas and institutions. And we are in this war, as we were in the last one, closely associated with them in the effort to defeat a common enemy. Nevertheless, many people in the United States are troubled by the idea that we are allied to an "imperialist" state (just as many others are troubled by the idea that we are allied with a "Communist" state) . They may admire the British and think well of the British Commonwealth of Nations; but there is for them something undercover and disingenuous about the British Empire. They may admit, even if somewhat grudgingly, that the British government is democratic. But why do the British, if they have a democratic government, have a king? And a king, moreover (and this is the real difficulty), who is Emperor of India? Forgetting that the United States rules alien people in Puerto Rico, Hawaii, and the Philippines, they ask why Great Britain, if it is really fighting for the freedom of all nations, does not immediately give India its freedom; and without asking President Roosevelt to abandon any of the overseas possessions of the United States, they find something Cliveden House and sinister in Mr. Churchill's frank statement that he did not become Prime Minister in order to preside at the dissolution of the British Empire.

It is for such superficial reasons as these that many people share Mr. Lindbergh's feeling that this war is no more than another clash of rival imperialisms, and applaud the statement attributed to Dorothy Thompson that she "would not lift a finger to save the British Empire as presently constituted." The statement (if Miss Thompson did, as reported, make it) reveals a strange inconsistency in thought and action. Miss Thompson may not have lifted a finger, but for many years now she has every week lifted her voice (and to very good purpose) to point out to the people of the United States the real nature of the Nazi political philosophy and practice, to arouse them to a proper sense of their danger from it, and to urge them to give all possible assistance to whatever countries are fighting to destroy it; and everything she has said and done to that end, every dollar spent and ship cleared by the United States to aid in the defeat of Hitler, has had the effect, whatever its intention may have been, to save the British Empire as it is now constituted.

Let us not be hypnotized and befuddled by words.

Let us say that Great Britain, Russia, China, and the United States are great imperial states, since that is what in fact they are. Let us admit, if it eases anyone's conscience, that they are "imperialistic" states. But let us place first things first, and judge imperial or imperialistic states by their works. It will then be seen that the imperialism which should now chiefly concern us is the imperialism of Germany and Japan. We can all agree that those particular manifestations of imperialism must be destroyed. We can all agree that the immediate aim of the present war is to destroy them; and the simple fact is that if we are now in a position to destroy them, it is because after the collapse of France the British Empire as now constituted was there, with its solid power, to carry on for twelve months single-handed a tenacious and successful resistance without which Hitler would long since have won the war.

The present moment is indeed a singularly inopportune time for the people of the United States, who cannot even repeal a poll tax designed to deprive Negroes of their rights as citizens, to cherish tender scruples about the purity of British imperialism. No doubt the British Empire has had, and still has, its faults and failures — as what great state has not? Certainly not the United States. But this may be said: in respect to political wisdom, restraint in the exercise of authority over alien people, and contribution to the spread of political freedom in the world, the British Empire does not suffer by comparison with any empire or great political power in ancient or modern times. The British Empire is a major political fact of our time, and should be judged, not by its isolated fail-

96

ures, but by its general achievements, not by what it has failed to do in the past but by what it is doing in the present crisis. So judged, one thing is, I should think, sufficiently obvious: if the political freedom which the British Empire guarantees and has long guaranteed in a large part of the world is to be preserved, if India is not to lose her present good prospect of obtaining a similar freedom and security, one essential thing for us to do now is to lift all our fingers to save the British Empire however constituted. How it may be constituted after the war is over we may well leave to the British and the people concerned, since we will undoubtedly, and rightly, expect them to leave to us the sufficiently difficult task of setting our own house in order.

3

It is said that we are fighting to preserve our political independence, but that after the war is over, the sovereign independence of states must be curbed. It is said that we are using our political power to destroy the political power of Germany and Japan, but that after the war is over power politics must be abandoned. It is said that after the war is over, imperialism must end and the white man must get out of the Far East, but that the great imperial white-man powers (the United States, Great Britain, and Russia) must co-operate with China in establishing and maintaining a durable peace in the Far East and throughout the world. It is said that in order to establish and maintain a durable peace in the world the four great powers must work together in harmony and good faith, but that they must at the same time "respect the right of all peoples to choose the form of government under which they will live."

These are all good aims, but the mere bald statement of them in this conjunction and contrast is sufficient to raise many fundamental and fundamentally embarrassing questions. Some of these questions will be considered later, but only two are relevant to the discussion at this point. The first is: Can the white-man powers get out of the Far East and at the same time co-operate effectively with China in maintaining a durable peace in the Far East? The second is: Can the great powers work together in harmony for maintaining a durable peace in the world and at the same time recognize the right of all peoples to choose the form of government under which they will live?

What exactly is meant by saying that the white man must get out of the Far East? I suppose it does not mean that the Australians must get out of the Far East, although the Australians are white men and Australia is in the Far East. I take it to mean that the white man must abandon political and military control of those Far Eastern countries that are chiefly inhabited by other people. If this is what is meant, then it would seem that the white man should also get out of the Near East and Africa, since these regions are likewise inhabited by other people. But if the white man must get out of the Far East after the war is over, the question may well be asked why not do it now when the going, with the competent aid of Japan, is so good? Why should the white man fight so desperately to stay in the Far East if the consequence of his retaining the power to stay in is that he should immediately get out?

This question may appear merely frivolous to many

liberal international idealists. But I think it entirely relevant to the situation, if for no other reason than that those who say that the white man must get out of the Far East after the war is over are mostly, as I suppose, altogether in favor of fighting the present war to a finish, and are now regretting, like the rest of us, that the white man did not get in more effectively before the war began — did not, that is to say, make himself impregnable in Singapore and the Straits, in the Dutch islands, in the Philippines and Hawaii. The reason for taking this view, they would no doubt say, is that the aggressive ambitions of Japan, united in purpose as they are with those of Germany, are a menace to the freedom and security of all freedom-loving peoples in Europe and America, in the Near and the Far East. For this reason the war must be fought to a finish and the power of Germany and Japan completely destroyed. But when the power of Japan, backed by Germany, is completely destroyed (so the argument seems to run), the menace to the freedom and security of China and the other nations of the Far East will be ended, and the white man (Russia, Great Britain, and the United States) can safely leave the Far East to the people who belong there — chiefly to the Chinese and the people of India.

Supposing the white man did this, what precisely would it mean? It would mean that Great Britain would withdraw her military and political power from India, Ceylon, North Borneo, the Straits Settlements, the Federated Malay States, Singapore, and Hong Kong; that Holland would withdraw from Java, Sumatra, Borneo, and other places inhabited by "peoples" totaling some sixty millions; that France would withdraw from Indo-China; that Russia would withdraw from all Asiatic possessions inhabited chiefly by non-Russians; and that the United States would withdraw from the Philippines and Hawaii. I do not think that any of these countries will make such a withdrawal. But supposing that Great Britain and the United States, feeling that with the destruction of Japanese power they were themselves safe, proposed to do so, I am wondering how safe the Chinese would feel. Would the Chinese welcome this method of co-operating with China for maintaining the peace of the Far East?

I do not know. But I should think that the Chinese, having maintained a desperate and heroic resistance against the senseless and barbarous oppression of the Japanese for six years (or will it be seven? Or eight?), would be well aware that although the power of Japan had been completely crushed, the Japanese would still be there, very close to them, waiting only for another opportunity to realize their aggressive ambitions. If I were a Chinese, that, I think, is what I should be most aware of, and I think I should feel much safer if Great Britain and the United States co-operated with my country in maintaining peace in the Far East by retaining a very considerable naval and air force there. The Chinese may wish the British to withdraw from Hong Kong, but will they wish them to withdraw from Singapore and the Straits? Will they wish the United States to weaken or to strengthen its naval and air force in the Philippines and Hawaii? We have offered the Filipinos independence, but do they want it now? Would the people of Hawaii wish the United States to withdraw and leave them to shift for themselves? And then there are the Australians. They also wish to live in peace and security within their own boundaries. But how secure would they feel, and how much peace would they look forward to, if Great Britain withdrew its naval and air force from the Far East and the United States abandoned the Philippines and Hawaii? The Australians, I feel sure, will think that a durable peace can be maintained in the Far East only if Great Britain and the United States greatly increase their naval and air forces in the Straits and at Singapore, in Hawaii and the Philippines, in New Guinea and the Solomon Islands — and any other strategic islands they may pick up during the present war.

Call the United States, Russia, and Great Britain what you like — great, imperial, imperialist powers. Whatever you call them, two things seem to me to be outside the realm of practical politics. One is that they will "give up" their sovereign independence, or allow it to be "curbed" except in so far as they may themselves be willing to curb it. The other is that they will withdraw their naval and air forces (that is to say, the guarantee of their political power) from the Far East. The only hope for a durable peace in the Far East is that these three imperial powers may be able to co-operate with each other and with China in establishing a settlement that will be satisfactory to them and to the innumerable and ill-defined "peoples" of India and the East India islands.

The only hope of establishing a durable peace in Europe is that Great Britain, Russia, a reconstituted France, and the United States can co-operate in harmony and good faith to establish and maintain a settlement that will be satisfactory to them and that does not create in Germany and Italy and the ill-defined nations of eastern Europe and the Near East a permanent and dangerous sense of oppression and inferiority

This brings us to the second question. Can the four great powers — Russia, Great Britain, a reconstituted France, and the United States — make and maintain a settlement that will take account of their several vital national interests (or what they regard as such) and at the same time recognize the right of all "nations" to live under governments of their own choosing.

It is visionary to suppose that these great powers will not have national interests which they regard as vital, or that these interests will not in some instances be in conflict. If they are to remain united in making and maintaining the peace of Europe, they will each have to make some concession to the interests of the others — in respect to Germany and Italy, in respect to the people of eastern Europe, the Near East, and northern Africa. In respect to Germany their interests need not be, so long as they stick together in other respects, in essential conflict. The United States, Russia, England, France, and the lesser countries of western Europe have a common interest in preventing any central great power from acquiring a dangerous ascendancy in Europe. None of these countries will recognize the right of Germans to live under a government of their own choosing if that right takes the form of another Nazi regime, or anything similar to it. The same is likely to be true in respect to the settlement of Italy. In respect to the defeated countries, therefore, the assumption that it is necessary for Russia, Great Britain, France, and the United States to remain united, if a durable peace is to be maintained, may or may not come into conflict with the assumption that it is in general desirable to "respect the right of all peoples to choose the form of government under which they will live." But what about the settlement of the other countries of Europe, of the Near East and northern Africa?

In respect to the settlement of the conquered and devastated countries of western Europe (France, Belgium, Holland, Denmark, and Norway) it is unlikely that any conflict of interests will arise between Russia, Great Britain, and the United States, or that there will be any difficulty in respecting the right of these peoples to choose the form of government under which they will live. These are all clearly defined and commonly recognized "nations," and they have for a long time lived within certain boundaries not often or much changed, and under governments of their own choosing. There are no serious boundary disputes between any of them; and neither Russia, Great Britain, nor the United States wants any of their territory or will object to the form of government they may wish to establish. In these countries, therefore, the political settlement will not give rise to insuperable difficulties, but in eastern Europe and perhaps in North Africa the political settlement will be far less simple.

In Poland, for example. Russia has already declared that she will retain certain parts of the Polish state as constituted in 1939. Just what people are comprised in the Polish "nation" is none too clear, and just what territory should by "historic right" be regarded as Polish is even less clear. But assuming that all of the people living under the Polish government in 1939 will after the war still wish to live under a Polish government of their own choosing, what should be the policy of the United States, Great Britain, and France in regard to the Polish settlement? Should they insist on applying the principle that all peoples be permitted to live under governments of their own choosing, and so run the risk of breaking with Russia? Or should they concede the demands of Russia, and thus to that extent abandon the principle of national self-determination? It would do them little good to insist on the principle if Russia refuses to accept it, since in eastern Europe Russia has not only the major interest but also the major power. It seems to me unlikely that either Great Britain, France, or the United States would risk a breach with Russia, and thus destroy the only hope of maintaining a durable peace in Europe, for the sake of the ideal principle of national self-determination — especially in a case in which neither the nation nor the territory belonging to it is clearly defined. What demands, if any, Russia may make in respect to the settlement in the Balkans is not known. But in all the states created by the Peace of Versailles bitter animosities between the various "national" groups, disputes among them for territorial possessions, and the certainty that there will be discontented minority groups whatever boundaries may be drawn are notorious and inescapable facts which will make it extremely difficult to apply the principle of national self-determination in any very satisfactory way.

In Africa the "imperial" interests that will interfere with any extended application of the principle
of national self-determination are not those of Russia, but those of France, Great Britain, and indirectly
the United States.

First of all, what are the "nations" of Africa? Egypt
is undoubtedly one, and since 1922 has been recognized as an independent sovereign state. Ethiopia is
undoubtedly another, and now that the Italians have
been driven out is again living under a government of
its own choosing. But the native inhabitants of Basu-
toland, Bechuanaland, Rhodesia, Swaziland, Kenya,
Nyanza, Tanganyika, Nyasaland, Somaliland, Nige-
ria, Gambia — are these so many separate nations,
and do they want Great Britain to withdraw and
allow them to live under governments of their own
choosing? Or the native inhabitants of French Congo,
the Cameroons, Somaliland, and the island of Mada-
gascar — are they so many separate nations, and do
they want the French to withdraw and allow them to
live under governments of their own choosing? Or,
disregarding the Negro tribes of central Africa, what
about the inhabitants of Libya, Algeria, Tunisia, and
Morocco? Do they regard themselves as separate nations, and do they wish to be entirely free from the
control and "protection" of any European country?

I am merely asking, I do not know enough about
any of these people to know the answers. But whatever the answers, I think it extremely unlikely that
Great Britain will be disposed to withdraw from any
part of Africa which she controlled before the war,
and unless she is willing to do so she will be in no
position to ask France to withdraw from the Congo,

the Cameroons, or even from Algeria, Tunisia, and
Morocco. In any case I do not think Great Britain will
wish France to withdraw from North Africa. Great
Britain, and the United States too, if they are wise,
will wish to have France as strong as possible, not only
as a necessary balance in Europe against Germany,
but as an indispensable aid to them in defending what
Walter Lippmann calls "the Atlantic community."
Whatever Great Britain and the United States may
want, unless I am much mistaken the French themselves, who have found their North African empire
the only place where they could gather their dispersed
political and military force for beginning the reconquest of their country and its political independence,
will think it the height of folly to abandon what has
served them so well in the most serious crisis in all
their history. Certainly in the present war the control
of North Africa has proved to be a crucial factor in
the defeat not only of Germany, but of Japan as well;
and I think it highly improbable that either France,
Great Britain, Russia, or the United States will consider that a durable peace can be maintained in the
world if the military defense and the political direction of North Africa are turned over entirely to the
politically weak nations of Libya, Algeria, Tunisia,
and Morocco. Is it even certain that the people of
North Africa would welcome the responsibility involved in so much freedom?

Such are some of the difficulties involved in any
attempt to apply the principle of the "right of all
peoples to choose the form of government under
which they will live." We cannot have it both ways.
If we urge the great powers to fight desperately in

order to preserve their political independence, and applaud them for doing it, we can hardly expect them to "give up" their political independence after the war is over. If we insist that the great powers remain united in order to establish and maintain a durable peace in the world, we must concede them the privilege of basing such a peace on what they regard as their vital interests and of using the power they have, and exerting the "pressure" needed at strategic points on the globe, to make and maintain it. At least that much "power politics" and "imperialism" will exist after the war is over, and will be the necessary condition of any new and better world. If it be said that the great states cannot be trusted with so much "uncurbed" power, the answer is that we must trust them with the power since they have it. It remains to be seen whether they can trust each other.

In that case, it will no doubt be asked: "What, then, are we fighting for? Are we fighting to preserve the status quo? A fair question. What *are* we fighting for?

5

What Are We Fighting For?

THIS QUESTION has been often asked, much discussed, and variously answered. There is what may be called the conventional answer, and there are what may be called the genuine answers. This distinction needs to be made clear.

There are various occasions in life in which one is expected to do and say certain conventional things. If your friend gets married you are expected to congratulate him, and you do so although you may really think he is making a frightful mistake. Or when an acquaintance dies you are expected to say: "That's too bad," or something of the sort, whereas you may be thinking: "and a good thing, too." When a country is at war the conventional thing to say is that it is defending itself against aggression, or fighting for the cause of freedom. That is now being said in all countries, the Axis countries as well as the others. We hear it every day over the radio and from the lecture platform, and read it in books and newspapers: "We are fighting for the preservation of our national independence, for the cause of human freedom, and for a new and better world." This is the conventional answer, which everyone expects to hear, and everyone, or almost everyone, accepts as a matter of course.

There are some exceptions. This is what an editorial writer in a New York newspaper has to say:

We are in the war on the side of Great Britain, and we
. . . must cooperate with the British in every possible way
to win the victory. . . . It is Mr. Churchill's invitation
to some sort of post-war union with Great Britain that
worries us. . . . We hope there will be no such post-war
union. We hope that after this war we shall cease to be in
effect a part of the British Empire, as we now are, and as
we were during our participation in World War I. . . .
If we are formally and officially hooked up with Britain
after this war . . . our power and resources will encour-
age them to . . . call us to new crusades. . . . Twice in
twenty-five years we have gone on such crusades.

This is as much as to say that twice in twenty-five
years we have been tricked into a war that was not
our affair. What are we fighting for? Well, if you ask
me, says this New York editor, we are fighting a useless crusade for getting Great Britain out of a mess.

There are no doubt a good many people who agree
with this, but not very many who come out frankly
and say so. Anyway the great majority accept the conventional answer, that we are fighting for the preservation of our independence and for the cause of human freedom. And they are for the most part entirely
sincere in thinking so. This is the answer that I my-
self give, and I think it the true answer. But there are
those in every country, more in some than in others
(it depends on how close the country has been brought
to the war), who accept this answer without thinking
much about it. They accept it because it is the proper
and decent answer — the thing which all good citizens and patriots are expected to think and say. When,
however, one talks with people "off the record," as

the newspaper men say, or reads books and pamphlets about the war and what is to come out of it, then it becomes clear that different people, whether they have thought much or little about it, mean different things when they say that we are fighting for human freedom and a better world after the war is over. These particular things that different people mean are their "genuine" answers to the question: What are we fighting for?

About the only thing that all people agree about is that we are fighting because we were "attacked" by Japan. For a great many people that is all they know or need to know. Having been attacked, there was nothing we could do but fight, and being in the war there is nothing we can do but win it. That is essentially what they mean by saying that we are fighting against aggression and for human freedom. If you should ask them why we needed to get Hawaii and the Philippines in the first place, and whether it wouldn't be better to let them go rather than sacrifice so many American lives, they would be simply puzzled or else think you crazy. Their answer would be: "Well, we got them anyway, and so we have to defend them, don't we? We couldn't take Pearl Harbor lying down. We gotta show the damn Japs where they get off." A sound enough answer as far as it goes, but of course it doesn't go very far in answering the question what are we fighting for.

It is much easier for most people to understand why we are fighting Japan than to understand why we are fighting Germany. Germany didn't "attack" us. Everyone has of course heard about *Mein Kampf* and the Nazi philosophy and practice, but for most people these things didn't mean very much before the war, and even now they don't mean as much as they might. Before the war some very good, quite ordinary people, who had not much knowledge of national or international affairs and no great interest in them, asked me if it really made much difference whether Hitler won the war — wouldn't things go on much the same for ordinary people? This was also the idea of the business tycoons who thought we could "do business with Hitler." Such people, big or little, probably have even yet no very clear notion of what Nazism really means. But they know that Germany and Japan are our enemies, and when their sons are in the war they can be proud of them, especially if they are decorated for bravery; and if their sons are killed in action they can feel with genuine conviction that they have died for their country and for human freedom. They naturally wish to feel that these American boys have not died in vain, and they can therefore say and believe that after the war something must be done to make a new and better world. Just what should be done is none too clear to them, and many will think that the world will be enough better if Germany and Japan are totally defeated. When the war is over, many of them will no doubt share the sentiment of the soldier on leave who said that when the war was won he wanted to return to the U.S.A. and "never hear of a foreign country again."

Then there are the leaders and molders of public opinion — politicians, business men, lawyers, doctors, clergymen, teachers in schools and professors in colleges, the writers of books, newspaper editors and columnists, and professional radio news commentators, and many intelligent people in every community who write no books and make no speeches but who read much and think seriously about the war and the peace. They are only a small minority of the nation, but they exert, in every community, an influence on opinion out of all proportion to their numbers.

Such leaders can tell us, and many of them do so at length, pretty definitely what they mean by saying that we are fighting for the preservation of our national independence and for the cause of human freedom. They generally agree that Germany and Japan must be totally defeated and the Nazi system totally destroyed, and that afterward something must be done to create a world in which nations can live in greater security and freedom. But they differ much as to just what can or should be done to achieve this end. Some think a world state impossible, others think it the only hope. Some think the main object is to prevent another war, and that a union of Great Britain, the United States, Russia, and China is sufficient for this, others think that unless there is a pretty radical change in international relations and in social organization we shall have "lost the peace" even though we have won the war.

To the question: What are we fighting for? there is thus no single or simple answer. It depends upon who the "we" are. The "we" includes many countries, and many groups within each country. The people who have been bombed and enslaved are more certain about what they are fighting for, and what they are fighting against, than the people of the United States, who, apart from soldiers and newspaper men at the front, have never seen a bomb drop and know nothing about the war except by hearsay. Moreover, people involved in the war get a more definite idea of what they are fighting for as the war goes on. Certainly the people of France and of England know much better now than they did in 1939 that they are fighting for the cause of human freedom. Perhaps, then, the best way to answer the question: What are we fighting for? is to go back to 1939 and see for what reasons various countries became involved in the war and how the progress of the war changed or clarified their ideas about what they are fighting for.

1

Looking back over the years from 1933 to 1938, it is easy to see that the "freedom-loving countries" could by united and decisive action before it was too late have stopped Hitler in his tracks and prevented the war. Of course it is always easy after a disaster has occurred to see what could and should have been done to prevent it. But with all allowances made for the superior wisdom of hindsight, it still seems incredible that England and France (to speak only of these freedom-loving countries) should have stood aside, as if from something that did not concern them, while Hitler established the Nazi system in Germany, built the most powerful army in the world, supported Mussolini in the brutal and senseless conquest of Ethiopia, aided Franco to destroy political freedom in Spain, and then proceeded to conquer and loot Austria and Czechoslovakia.

There are of course explanations of this indifference to their own safety and the cause of human freedom. One is that the responsible leaders of these countries did not know how vile and dangerous a thing the Nazi system was. Another is that they could not believe that Hitler meant what he said when he told the world frankly in *Mein Kampf* just what he intended to do and how he intended to do it. Still another is that they did believe that Hitler meant what he said when he promised never to demand any European territory except that inhabited by Germans. None of these explanations is adequate. Responsible leaders had little excuse for not knowing what Nazism or Fascism really was, both in theory and in practice. For years both Hitler and Mussolini had been explaining, clearly if blatantly, that Nazism and Fascism were systematic organizations of force and fraud, and for years both had exhibited the theory in action. The ruthless suppression of all political freedom, of freedom of thought and of teaching and learning, the systematic liquidation of the Jews, the official glorification and inculcation of hate and brutality, the concentration camps, in which the most degrading torture was authorized and practiced — it was all there, explained in writing and recorded in deeds, for all the world to look at. A few people, even a few in high position, such as Ambassador Dodd and Winston Churchill, saw what they looked at and understood what it meant. But the responsible leaders of the freedom-loving countries were either too stupid to understand or too indifferent to care. Mostly too stupid. Certainly nothing could have been more stupid than to suppose, as late as 1937, that Hitler did not mean what he said in *Mein Kampf,* unless it was to suppose that he did mean what he said at Berchtesgaden and Munich.

The perfect and classic example of this stupidity is recorded, unconsciously, in the book entitled *The*

Fighting For?

Failure of a Mission, by the late Sir Nevile Henderson, British Ambassador to Germany in the years immediately before the war. Henderson was an educated English gentleman, sent to Germany to make himself agreeable to the Nazi leaders in order to find out what they wanted, what they would be satisfied with, and to impress upon them the desirability of preserving peace in Europe. Sir Nevile made himself agreeable and did his best to carry out his instructions, but his mission failed. The principal failure recorded in his book, however, is the failure of Henderson's mind to understand what was going on in Germany or the real character of the persons responsible for it. With every chance to see what was going on, he saw nothing that was very shocking. With every opportunity to see and talk with Hitler, Goebbels, and Goering, he found nothing in them to be much alarmed about. He thought Hitler a man of great force — an odd fellow certainly, but then foreigners were apt to be odd fellows. He thought Goebbels a shrewd and intelligent man. He saw more of Goering than of anybody else, and thought him rather of the blustering and bragging sort, but after all, in the naïve and vain German way, human and rather jolly. He enjoyed Goering's lavish hospitality and liked the man as much as an English gentleman could like a hearty fellow. They were all an odd lot, but not so bad as they were painted; and Henderson returned to England without ever learning that Hitler, Goebbels, and Goering were not, under their rough exteriors, men of honor whose promises could be trusted, or that the Nazi system was anything more than a pretty arbitrary government which Englishmen would not find agreeable.

Henderson was an ideal representative of the ideas and the policy of the British Prime Minister, Neville Chamberlain. In their training, their abilities, their virtues, and their defects the two men were much alike. Chamberlain wanted desperately to prevent war, both because he knew it would be an unparalleled calamity and because he believed that the outcome, whatever it was, would provide a fertile field for the propagation of Russian Communism. His policy for preventing war was what is called "appeasement" — the policy of conceding as much as possible to Hitler in the expectation that he would be satisfied with a Germany that would include all the territories inhabited by Germans.

In 1938, when Hitler demanded the German (Sudeten) lands of Czechoslovakia, Chamberlain therefore took the unprecedented step of flying to Germany for a personal conference with Hitler at Berchtesgaden. There he was much applauded by the people and received in state by the government. Like Henderson, he also thought Hitler an odd fellow, because he got excited, and ranted instead of talking over matters in a quiet way as gentlemen and statesmen should. Nevertheless, he got promises from Hitler which he thought satisfactory, and flew again to Godesberg. But of course Hitler made further demands, and threatened to march his army into Czechoslovakia on October 1 if the demands were not accepted. This was followed by the hastily arranged conference (at Munich, September 29) between Hitler, Mussolini, the French Premier, Daladier, and Chamberlain. There it was agreed that the Sudeten lands in which the Germans were a majority should be ceded to Germany, and that in certain other regions the people should decide the matter by plebiscite. Both the French and the Russian governments had assured the Czechs that they would support Czechoslovakia against German aggression, but neither the French nor the British government was willing to risk a war, and the Czechs were therefore notified that they must accept the Munich agreement. Chamberlain came home from Munich much elated — returned, as he said, "with honor" and "peace for our time."

No more disastrous mistake was ever made by a British statesman. At Munich Hitler had promised that he would never demand any more European territory; but he had insisted that as a guarantee of the performance of the terms of the Munich Pact the German army should be permitted to make a peaceful march into Czechoslovakia. The Czechs were not deceived. They knew that the Munich Pact was a farce, and so it proved to be. Once in Czechoslovakia, the Germans took possession. Within six months Slovakia was erected into a separate but puppet German state, and Bohemia and the greater part of Moravia were annexed to Germany. The Czech political and intellectual leaders who did not escape were sent to concentration camps or executed. The country was systematically looted. Landed property was transferred by forced contract to Germans, and it is said that the original records of title were destroyed. Food and the products of industry and the contents of museums and libraries were loaded into hundreds of stolen trucks and taken to Germany. Schools and universities were purged of Czech teachers or closed altogether. University students, men and women, were taken at night from their lodgings and herded by the Gestapo into a public square for a routine exhibition of sadism. The young men were beaten and tortured into insensibility, revived by douches of cold water, and again tortured into insensibility or death; and in the meantime, as a needed relaxation, the young women were publicly and repeatedly raped, the members of the Gestapo queuing up, each man waiting his turn, all to the accompaniment of much libidinous laughter and hilarity

The Czechs did not need to learn about Nazism from books. They saw it in action and experienced its effects. They knew at first hand what Nazism was, and it wasn't anything that a civilized people could do business with or appease. They knew without any doubt what they were fighting for, and it wasn't anything that could be preserved or recovered by conference discussions with Hitler, or nice calculation of the national interest, or diplomatic maneuvering for a favorable adjustment of the balance of power. They knew they were fighting for their national existence and their political freedom, and for something more fundamental even than these — the elemental decencies of any civilized living. And they knew that if Europe was ever again to be a place where civilized men could endure to live, the freedom-loving countries would have to subordinate all class conflicts and national interests to the immediate and common task of crushing Hitler and his Nazi supporters as one would root out and destroy a nest of oversized rattlesnakes.

The people of France and England did not learn

this until later, but the destruction of Czechoslovakia convinced them that Hitler's pledged word was worthless, and that since he could not be stopped by appeasement he had to be stopped by force. When, therefore, Hitler began the same tactics against Poland that he had used against Czechoslovakia, France and Great Britain agreed to come to the aid of Poland with all their forces if the Polish government found it necessary to resist German aggression by force. In accord with this agreement they declared war on Germany on September 3, 1939.

The Polish treaty was in the nature of a diplomatic pretext. Neither Great Britain nor France declared war on Germany in order to preserve democratic government in Poland — there was no democratic government in Poland to preserve — nor in the hope of saving Poland from immediate conquest, since for geographical reasons it was impossible for them to give Poland any direct military aid. They declared war on Germany in order to stop Hitler from acquiring an ascendancy in Europe which would endanger their security and might endanger their political independence. It was for them a Hobson's choice — not a choice between peace and war, but between war then or later; and they chose not to wait because they had waited too long as it was, and to delay any longer would only give Hitler greater advantages than he already had. They declared war in order to safeguard their own interests by redressing the balance of power against Hitler and in their own favor.

Poland was soon conquered, and partitioned between Germany and Russia, and the German part looted and devastated with even more systematic and brutal inhumanity than Czechoslovakia had been. For eight months there was virtually no fighting on the western front, and no adequate preparation made by either France or Great Britain for waging the kind of war that Hitler was prepared to wage. Then, in May 1940, came the rapid conquest, without pretext or notification, of Denmark, Norway, Holland, and Belgium; the defeat of the French-British armies, and the disastrous retreat of the British from Dunkirk; the conquest and subjugation of France, and the terrific bombing of Britain. Then it was that the people of all these countries learned what Nazism was really like and what the war was really about. The people of Norway, Denmark, Holland, and Belgium learned that a policy of isolation, a policy of relying on the balance of power and the accepted rules for conducting war, was of no avail. The rich industrialists and intriguing civil and military politicians of France learned the incredible folly of supposing that Hitler might be a lesser evil than "socialism," and the working classes learned that this was after all something more than a "rich man's war" that did not concern them. Then it was that the British people learned that they were fighting, not merely for redressing the balance of power against a too strong Germany, but for the complete destruction of the Nazi state as totally incompatible with any sort of political independence or freedom in Europe or in the world at large. The Russian people learned all this as soon as their country was invaded by the Nazi armies; the people of Ethiopia, Spain, and China had already learned it before the European war began.

2

The people of the United States are learning about Nazism and the nature of the war by the same process, but, since the experience is far less drastic, more slowly; and it is unlikely that they will ever learn it as effectively as the people of Europe and of China have learned it. We were told what the Japanese did in China, what the Spanish-Italo-German Fascists did in Spain, and what the German Nazis did in Czechoslovakia and Poland; but we did not really take it in, any more than the French and British people took it in before 1940. It was all too remote from us — a story of events happening far away, to be read about and deplored. However deplorable, these remote events were not our affair, we thought at first, and we determined to keep out of the war and avoid its effects by refusing to fight other people's battles, by refusing even to defend our own neutral rights. But after the collapse of France, when it seemed likely that Britain would be conquered too, we realized that the preservation of the British Empire was of some importance to us; and we then entered the war in effect by adopting the policy of "Lend-Lease," the policy of "giving all aid short of war" — all aid short of the essential aid. We entered the war formally and with all aid only when we were forced in by the Japanese attack on Pearl Harbor and the Philippines. We entered the war, in short, as France and Great Britain had done, for the defense of our national interests; and we are still (October 1943) fighting it on that ground. We are thoroughly united in believing that the war must be fought to a finish; and we are told every day, and we believe sincerely enough, that we are fighting for human freedom against German and Japanese barbarism. But we still do not realize, as the people of Europe and China realize, what that barbarism can mean to those who have experienced it.

We realize it effectively only in so far as it touches us directly. To those who have much imagination it seems that we should do better than that. The murder of some of Doolittle's men, says Mr. Norman Cousins, had an effect on the United States that

revealed . . . a significant aspect of the American relation to the war. The news broke upon a stunned and bewildered nation. America was as incredulous as it was horrified, as shocked as it was outraged. It seemed inconceivable that the laws of warfare, such as they are, should be so brazenly violated. . . .

It is one thing to be outraged, and another to be surprised. Why were we so surprised, so incredulous? Where have we been all these years when the same thing was happening on a vastly larger scale? What were we dreaming about when thousands of Chinese soldiers and civilians were killed by Japanese gas attacks? . . . Where were the American headlines when the Japanese themselves announced, only two days after they boasted of the execution of the American fliers, that the occupants of the Chinese villages near the place where the American fliers were forced down were also murdered? These people were guilty of the crime of geography: their miserable little homes happened to be in the vicinity of the landings, so they were put to death, thousands of them. It is almost a game. Some call it Kwangtu. Others call it Lidice. Take a pin and stick it in the map — anywhere, it makes no difference. That gives you the place. Next you devise means of putting the people to death. Shall they be lined up and shot? Or perhaps that would be too expensive. Maybe they can be crowded under a single roof and set afire. That would cost less, and the people would squirm more. For the next game, you can round up all people who live in odd-numbered houses and tear out their fingernails.

There is nothing far-fetched about this. The only thing that is far-fetched and inexplicable is our own inability to hear the thunder unless and until it breaks over our own heads. Nothing really happens until it happens to us.

This is only too true. But it is quite as true of other people as it is of us. What happened to the Ethiopians, the Spanish, the Czechs, the Poles, didn't happen *for* the French and the British until it happened *to* them. None of it, not even the ordinary effects of war, has as yet happened to us, and so, except for persons as sensitive and imaginative as Mr. Cousins, it hasn't happened. Not really, not so that we can act as if it had. It is not that we are less sensitive or imaginative than other people, or less affected by what is barbarous and inhumane; it is only that we are more remote from the war. We have been in the war for nearly two years, and we have contributed enormously and willingly to the winning of it. But apart from the men at the front, we do not see the war or suffer any of its effects.

The war is not being, and will not be, fought on our soil. Our national independence, although indirectly threatened, is not in any serious danger, and no one thinks it is. We try to simulate raids, and to stimulate our imagination, by having blackouts. But no hostile plane has been sighted, no bomb dropped, not the meanest shanty destroyed; and so a good lady can refuse to turn out her lights because she believes in God and knows that he will protect us. Apart from the soldiers at the front and the people whose sons have died, we do not suffer from the war, we are not even inconvenienced by it. Not really. Our gas is rationed, and we know the reason for it; but still we clamor for more gas and even as it is we drive our cars far more than is necessary. Our food is rationed, but as a nation we are better fed than we were before the war, and our garbage cans are no less full. No one suffers from want, no one goes hungry — except for that second pat of butter, or customary roast lamb, or favorite dry wine. No one suffers from loss of political freedom, or freedom to shoot off his mouth. No one slinks about in fear of spies and secret police. No one has seen the inside of a concentration camp, or been beaten up, or had his house looted by the Gestapo. Of Quisling and Gauleiters, of burning villages, of systematic and sadistic torture inflicted for the fun of it — of all this we know nothing at first hand, and will know nothing.

We are fighting for national independence and for human freedom, but not with the same profound conviction, the same singleness of purpose, or the same willingness to make sacrifices for the common good as the people who have lost, or have been near losing, these good things. And so quite good ladies can fill their basements with food in order not to be guilty of hoarding when the time comes, and quite good men can try to beat the gas racket, and politicians can play politics and beef about irrelevancies, and newspaper editors can indulge in the incredible stupidity

124

of supposing that we have been tricked into the war in order to get Britain out of a mess, and grave Solons can childishly demand that the fleet be brought home in order to protect California or New England against German or Japanese submarines that might conceivably pop a few small shells into the coast towns.

This brief survey of how certain countries became involved in the war and what they learned from experience about it throws some light perhaps on the question: What are we fighting for? In general terms we may answer the question as follows. We, the people of the United Nations, are fighting (those who are fighting — a good number are not fighting at all) for a common purpose — for the preservation or recovery of national independence, and for the cause of human freedom, against the Nazi barbarism, whether of the German or the Japanese variety. The people of those countries that have been devastated and despoiled by Nazi barbarism certainly know better than the others what they are fighting *against,* and for that reason they perhaps know somewhat better what they are fighting *for.* But at all events they are all fighting primarily for the preservation of something they have or the recovery of something they have lost — their native soil, their national independence, their familiar institutions and way of life. In this sense they are all fighting for the cause of human freedom. But it is not for human freedom in the abstract, or for some imagined but non-existent ideal freedom, that they are fighting. On the contrary, each country is fighting for the particular sort of freedom — the particular set of political and social institutions —

with which it is familiar and to which it is attached. They are all fighting, in short, for the preservation of what they had before the war began.

I was on the point of saying that they are all fighting for the preservation or the restoration of the status quo ante; but "status quo" is a fighting term. Better not use it without smiling, or at least without explaining what one means by it.

3

The term "status quo," like the terms "power politics" and "imperialism," is now in ill repute. I get the impression, from what I hear in certain circles and read in certain books and journals, that to say a good word for the status quo is equivalent to betraying the New Deal, or giving aid and comfort to Mr. Hoover, or to those others who nightly bow their heads in solemnity to say a prayer of hate against President Roosevelt. I have even heard in conversation and read in print the statement that if the war does no more than to preserve the status quo it will have been fought in vain.

I confess I do not understand what this statement, taken at its face value, can possibly mean. It seems to me equivalent to saying that the owner of a solid but somewhat run-down old house, finding the house in flames and laboring desperately to put out the fire, will have labored in vain if he does nothing more than to preserve the structure, with its outmoded plumbing and heating system, as a possible habitation. He has at least saved the house and can go on living in it: whether he thoroughly repairs it and puts in up-to-date plumbing or not, he has at least preserved the better part of what he had, which was a sensible thing to do, and the primary purpose of all his effort.

I have much admiration, and some sympathy, for the author writing in the New York *Times,* who stuck his neck out in defense of the status quo. He made no bones about it.

What is this America that we are now fighting to defend? For more than a year after the collapse of France England alone held the gate against Hitler. Without the English stand America would have had no time to become the arsenal of democracy. But without the good hope of American aid England might have been unequal to the mighty task. We are the hope of the world today in the sense that we have the final say. We have the casting vote for victory, and we have cast it for humanity and civilization.

That is the kind of America people are asked to defend — the old hope, the old record. When our young people a few years ago envied the flaming faith in the hearts of Hitler's and Mussolini's young men, did they happen to note the identity of the country to which the victims of Hitler's and Mussolini's crusading faith were fleeing for refuge? The refugees came to America, as the refugees have been coming to America for more than 300 years. The victims of the Hitler terror did not stipulate for a better America before they consented to seek refuge here. Our old American Status Quo was plenty good enough for them. Our old American Status Quo gave them life, liberty and livelihood.

What, then, do we seriously mean that America of the 12,000,000 unemployed ten years ago is the hope of the world? Yes.

America of the Economic Royalists and utility pirates the hope of the world? Yes.

America of the Ku Klux fanatics, of the Negro lynchings, of the Dillingers and the corrupt politicians — this America the hope of the world? Yes.

One need not take America's word for it. Ask the people of Britain, Russia, China and the conquered and martyred nations of Europe what they think of the American record.

This writer does not, I suppose, wish to preserve the status quo in all respects. I suppose he wishes as much as anyone to get rid of unemployment, utility pirates, Ku Klux Klan fanatics, Negro lynchings, corrupt politicians, and all the rest of it. But he has the sense to see these things in perspective, as undesirable aspects of the status quo which certainly no one wishes to preserve, in their proper relation to the fundamental aspects of the status quo which most of us certainly do wish to preserve. In talking about the new and better world, and still more in trying to make one, it is highly important not to lose sight of, or fail to take into account, the status quo as a whole, its fundamental virtues as well as its superficial defects.

The primary purpose of this war, unless I am completely mistaken, is to preserve the status quo in its fundamentals, even if that involves preserving its superficial defects. We are certainly (everyone says so) fighting to preserve our American way of life. And what are the fundamentals of our way of life? They are what they have always been since 1789 — the sovereign political independence of the United States; the system of representative government as defined in the Constitution: free economic enterprise tempered by such social regulation as from time to time seems to be essential; and the constitutional guarantees of the right of the individual to freedom from arbitrary arrest and imprisonment, freedom to choose one's occupation and to be secure in it, freedom of religion, of speech and the press, and of learning and teaching. Imperfectly realized these freedoms are, certainly; and certainly the system of government is capable of improvement. But this system of government and these freedoms, such as they are, are what we have. They are the fundamentals of the status quo. And they are what we are fighting to preserve.

In the world at large, before the war began, the status quo was a group of independent sovereign states, more or less powerful, and within each state a social and political system such as the people wished, or could manage to establish: a system of government in many countries somewhat similar to our own, in others very different from our own. The nations conducting the war against Germany and Japan, and the conquered and devastated countries in so far as they are able, are now fighting to preserve where it exists, and to restore where it has been destroyed, this system of sovereign independent states and the privilege of the people in each state to "choose the form of government under which they will live." It is the Axis powers that have destroyed in part, and would if they could completely destroy, the status quo. If the United Nations defeat the Axis powers they will certainly not have fought the war in vain: they will at least have preserved the better part of what they had. Whether they will also "win the peace," whether they will be disposed or able to use their victory to "afford to all nations the means of dwelling in safety within their own boundaries," to further "the enjoyment of all states . . . to access, on equal terms, to the trade and raw materials of the world," and to "bring about the collaboration of all nations in the economic field . . . for securing . . . improved labor standards, economic adjustments, and social security" — whether and to what extent they can do all this remains to be seen. But if they do not first win the war and preserve the status quo as a starting-point, there is not the slightest chance that any of these things will be done, or even attempted.

In one sense, of course, and a very real sense too, there is no status quo — no fixed set of institutions and laws and customs which any society can preserve or to which it can ever return. Institutions and customs are always changing because the conditions under which men live are always changing. In normal times such changes are relatively slow and occur so inconspicuously that hardly anyone pays any attention to them. The invention of the automobile, for example, gradually and insidiously changed the methods of travel and transportation. Dirt roads gave way to macadam and concrete roads. Interurban streetcar lines went bankrupt, and railroads lost much of their business because trucks carried so much freight. Certain kinds of crimes increased because criminals could get about more rapidly and more secretly. Suburban property increased in value because people could live ten or twenty miles from the place where they worked. And so on. In a thousand ways the customs and behavior of people were modified by the coming of the automobile.

In times of "revolution" (and war is a species of revolution) the normal rate of change is accelerated; and if the revolution is deliberately planned and directed to a definite end, the changes in laws and institutions may be far-reaching. But at best, or worst, less is accomplished than was intended. Tradition — the complex pattern of thought and conduct carried over from the past — is a tough and resistant thing; and I do not know of any successful attempt to break with the past and start afresh. The French Revolution of 1789 was a deliberate attempt to effect a radical transformation of the structure of French society, and within six years it made some pretty drastic changes in social and economic institutions and in the form of government. But the Jacobin dream of discarding the past, of beginning over again with the Year I, of destroying Christianity and of creating a Reign of Virtue based on a new religion of humanity — all this was defeated. The Russian Revolution of 1917 was also deliberately planned, and it also made some drastic changes in Russian institutions. It liquidated the "capitalist" class and nationalized private property in land and industry. But the Communist dream of creating a classless society, of destroying nationalist sentiment, of curbing the sovereign state, and of discarding the national interest as a guiding principle for the conduct of international relations — all this was likewise defeated. In both cases the past was too strong to be discarded; and twenty years after the great upheaval the social structure in each case owed more to history than it did to the revolution.

Human nature cannot all at once be greatly modified, or the dominant trends of historical development in essentials be reversed or sharply diverted, by good resolutions or plans the most efficient and carefully considered. And after all we should be glad of it. For it is the tough resistance of the status quo — the persistence of tradition, the force of national sentiment, loyalty to the sovereign state, attachment to established institutions and cherished customs — that is defeating and will completely defeat the stupendous effort of Nazi Germany, supported by the most efficient organization and the most scientific and ruthless application of power ever seen, to abolish the status quo and to create a new order in Europe on the ruins of the old.

The immediate effect of the collapse of Germany and Japan is impossible to predict. In Europe it may be a condition of political and economic chaos, of hunger and desolation, unknown since the Thirty Years' War. The recovery, fortunately, will be much more rapid because the victorious nations will find it necessary, for reasons of interest as well as of humanity, to establish some sort of political authority and economic order as rapidly as possible. With the collapse of Japan a similar restoration will be necessary in the Far East. How long this will take, either in Europe or in the Far East, is uncertain. Precisely what alterations in former boundaries or forms of government may be found necessary is also uncertain. But when the period of military occupation is ended, the political organization of the world will emerge, like the hills and streams of a countryside after being choked and devastated by a hurricane, much the same in its essential features as it was before. As before, there will be a few great states and many secondary or small states; for the most part they will be the same states as before the war; and in the majority of these states the social and political structure will be in essentials what it was. In all essentials this will be a restoration of the status quo — the preservation of what we had.

This restored national and international system (call it the status quo or what you like) will be what we have to start from in making a new and better world. The new and better world, which we should certainly all work for, must be firmly grounded on the old. It cannot by any miracle or magic be created all at once. In the effort to win new and better-secured freedoms, governments will again be confronted with the two problems which have baffled them for more than fifty years. Neither problem will be essentially different from what it was before, or any less difficult of solution. Within the nations there will be the old problem of "social security" — the problem of a maximum production and a more equitable distribution of wealth. In the world at large there will be the old problem of devising means for an orderly and satisfactory adjustment of international disputes, for promoting international trade and cultural relations, and for preventing war.

The two problems are intimately related, and no country can deal with either to good advantage without taking the other into account. But for purposes of discussion it is convenient to take them separately, and in the next chapter I will discuss the first one under the caption: What kind of collectivism do we want?

6

What Kind of Collectivism Do We Want?

MOST PEOPLE in the United States would probably answer this question by saying: "We do not want any kind of collectivism at all." The word "collectivism" is apt to suggest the word "socialism," and Socialism is for most people the same thing as Communism. This mistake leads to a great deal of useless confusion in thinking about such matters. First of all, therefore, I wish to make perfectly clear what I mean by collectivism. By collectivism I mean no more than the governmental regulation or control of the economic life of a community. Such regulation or control may be more or less complete, so that there are different kinds of collectivism, depending on the extent to which the regulation or control is carried out and the methods by which it is achieved. To say that we do not want any kind of collectivism is merely to express a pious wish. It is not a question of what we should like if it were possible to have it, but a question of what we must accept under conditions as they exist. We already have a certain amount of collectivism, a certain amount of governmental regulation of economic life; and it is about as clearly on the cards as anything can be that we must have still more of it.

But why must we have more of it? Why can't we have what we want? This raises the interesting ques-

134

tion which philosophers have discussed from time out of mind: Do men make their own history, or is it made for them by some power over which they have no control? The proper answer is that neither part of the question can be answered wholly in the affirmative. Men make their own history in part, and in part it is made for them by certain conditions which they cannot change, or cannot altogether change.

One of these conditions is physiographic — conditions of geography, soil, climate, and the like. Men can raise rice and bananas, but it would be a waste of effort to try to raise them in Labrador or New England. The other condition is historic — the pattern of habits and customs and institutions that exists at any time and place as the result of a long process of historical development. Men living in New England today can have all the rice and bananas they want, because these foods can now be so easily and cheaply brought to New England from the places where they are raised. But modern methods of transportation are part of the complex pattern of habit and institutions which has been historically created; and this complex pattern of habit and institutions is itself a limitation which determines in part the power of men to make their own history. It has been said that we should be better off if there were no steam engines, automobiles, or airplanes. Maybe we should. But the fact is that we have these things. We cannot get rid of them by wishing; and we can make our own history from now on only within the limits set by the existence and use of steam engines, automobiles, and airplanes, and the kind of society which these and a thousand and one other technological devices make necessary.

The pattern of thought and behavior, of customs and institutions that exist at any time can be changed by men, but not easily or all at once; and the way in which it can be changed, and the direction which the change must take, are as much determined by what has occurred and what exists as they are by men's will and desire. During the last century social and political institutions, and men's ways of thinking about them, have been changing, at times pretty rapidly; but they have been changing in a certain direction. This direction, the historical trend of our time, has been steadily away from unrestrained "private economic enterprise" and towards governmental regulation of private economic enterprise — that is to say, towards some form of what I have defined as collectivism.

Four different forms of collectivism have in fact been proposed or adopted — Socialism, Communism, Fascism, and what for lack of a better term we may call Social Democracy. We cannot reverse the historic trend towards collectivism, but we can with intelligence and determination decide whether we will have some brand of Social Democracy rather than some brand of Socialism, Communism, or Fascism. It will clarify the issue to see how these various brands of collectivism emerged historically, in what respects they are alike, and in what respects they are different.

1

The various forms of collectivism have emerged during the last hundred years. They are all methods proposed or adopted for solving the social and political problems arising in the highly complex societies cre-

136

ated by the Industrial and Technological Revolution
of our time; and a brief historical sketch will serve
to show what the nature of the problem is and how
these forms of collectivism propose to solve it.

Modern democracy, in theory and as in fact established, was the result of opposition to the system of
society and government that existed in most European
countries in the seventeenth and eighteenth centuries. Most countries were then governed by kings who
claimed absolute power by divine right, and whose
power in fact rested upon the support of a small but
influential class of privileged nobles, a few wealthy
middle-class families, and an established state church,
Protestant or Catholic. The mass of the people (chiefly
peasant farmers) were oppressed and exploited and
had few rights as we understand them — neither political freedom, nor freedom of religion, or of speech
and the press, nor freedom to choose one's occupation
or profession. Except in England, Holland, and the
American colonies, citizens had no safeguard against
arbitrary arrest and imprisonment, no right to trial
by jury, no protection against search of their houses
and possessions by the police. It was what we should
call a highly "regimented" society governed by heredi-
tary dictatorship. The English Revolution of 1688,
and the American and French Revolutions at the end
of the eighteenth century, were directed against this
form of dictatorship, class privilege, and social regi-
mentation; and by the end of the nineteenth century
it had been replaced in most European countries and
in America by some form of Liberal Democracy.

The theory or philosophy of Liberal Democracy
was formulated in the seventeenth and particularly in

the eighteenth century in a multitude of books and pamphlets, even though the authors ran the risk of having their works suppressed and of being themselves imprisoned or exiled. The classic expression of the philosophy is in the Declaration of Independence, written by Thomas Jefferson, and in the French Declaration of the Rights of Man and the Citizen, which was prefixed to the first French Constitution in 1789. The philosophy rested on the assumption that men had been too much and, above all, too arbitrarily governed. It was thought, rightly enough, that the chief oppressions and injustices from which men suffered were the result of governmental restraints upon the activities and thinking of men; and "liberty" was accordingly thought of as freedom for the individual from the restraints imposed by governments. The fundamental idea of the liberal democratic philoso-. phy, therefore, was that the people could govern themselves better than kings and aristocrats and priests could do it for them; and that the best form of government was the one that governed least — the one that interfered as little as might be with the activities and thinking of the individual citizen. In the early ninteenth century writers on economics used two French words to express this idea — *laissez* (let) and *faire* (to do or to be) . That is to say, governments should adopt the policy of *laissez faire* — should, as far as possible, let every man do what he wanted to do and be what he wanted to be. As applied to government, the philosophy might be called the do-nothing philosophy, and as applied to the citizen, the let-alone philosophy.

Of course this is putting it too baldly. There never

was a time when anyone (except a few philosophical anarchists, such as Proudhon) believed that governments should do nothing, or that citizens should be allowed to do as they please. But in the early and middle nineteenth century it was the prevailing belief that governments should not "meddle in business." The sole duty of government, it was thought, was to protect life and property, maintain civil order, and safeguard the country against foreign aggression. All citizens would then be free to engage in whatever profession or occupation they preferred, and each man would find his natural level of ability and do the job he was best fitted to do. In that case the natural desire of everyone to make money and get on in the world would result in the maximum of effort and efficiency, and therefore in the maximum production of wealth; and free competition, keeping prices at the lowest possible level, would result in as equitable a distribution of wealth as the natural abilities and defects of men permitted. The general idea was that if each man attended to his own individual interests, a kind of harmony of all the several interests in the nation would more or less automatically emerge. "Private profit is a public benefit" — so the idea was briefly expressed.

This simple theory of *laissez faire,* of every man for himself and devil take the hindmost, would always work to the advantage of the strong against the weak. Even in the relatively simple societies of the eighteenth and the early nineteenth century it would work to the advantage of those few who by good fortune, superior intelligence, or lack of scruple were able to acquire wealth and use it to further their selfish interests by means of political "pressure": there would always be a sufficient number of not-too-good men to come to the aid of the party. But with the coming of power-driven machinery it soon became evident that unrestrained competition in industry would not work as well as economists and political philosophers thought it would. In England, in the 1830's, the manufacture of cotton cloth by the new machines was a most profitable industry. It was profitable, however, only to the owners of the industry and of the machines that did so much of the work. It was the reverse of profitable to the laborers, who had no share in the ownership or management of the industry and were forced to accept whatever wages the employers might offer. And since there were more laborers wanting jobs than could be employed, the owners of the industry had it all their own way, and the laborers found that freedom to choose their own occupation was limited to the necessity of working long hours for starvation wages at any job that might turn up.

The situation in the cotton factories became so scandalous that Parliament appointed a committee to investigate it. The members of the committee were appalled by what they found; and it is said that they decided not to mention the worst things for fear that if they did no one would believe anything they said. Even so, the conditions as reported by the committee were such as would not now be tolerated — underfed, anemic women and children working twelve hours a day, in foul, unsanitary, and dangerous shops, for wages that would barely sustain life. The public conscience was shocked by the report; and in 1833 Parliament passed an act to improve matters a little. The act provided that no children under nine years of age should be employed in factories; and that the hours of labor for children from nine to thirteen years should be limited to forty-eight hours per week, and for children from thirteen to eighteen years to sixty-nine hours per week.

Children nine years of age working eight hours a day, children fourteen years of age working twelve and a half hours a day — this was thought to be an improvement! And it was for that time. But the point is that this first "Factory Act" was passed on the ground that government must "meddle in business" in order to protect laborers who were not in a position to bargain on equal terms with employers. The further point is that this first Factory Act was only a beginning. From 1833 to the present time the English government has been constantly and increasingly "meddling in business," has passed innumerable laws designed to correct manifest injustices growing out of free competition in private business enterprise — laws relating to child labor, to hours of labor and to wages, to labor unions and strikes and collective bargaining, laws requiring employers to provide sanitary conditions in factories and making them responsible for accidents to laborers, laws basing taxation on ability to pay, and the like. Similar laws have been passed in other countries. Before Hitler came with his mania for destroying every good thing, Germany had what was regarded as the most comprehensive and the best code of social insurance in the world. Few countries have gone farther than Holland, Denmark, Norway, and Sweden in the regulation of private business enterprise for the purpose of equalizing opportunities and possessions. The United States, because of the easier conditions of life, has lagged behind European countries in this respect. But in 1873 laws were passed to protect farmers against excessive and unfair freight rates charged by the railroads; and the courts upheld the laws on the ground that "the state must be permitted to adopt such rules and regulations as may be necessary for promoting the general welfare of the people." Since then many laws have been passed in restraint or for the regulation of free competition in order to achieve for the mass of the people what Theodore Roosevelt called a "Square Deal," what Woodrow Wilson called the "New Freedom," and what Franklin Roosevelt called the "New Deal."

Many people seem to think that the New Deal is something brand-new. It is obviously not something new, but merely an acceleration of a trend that has been going on for a long time. In all democratic countries for the last seventy-five or one hundred years there has been an increasing amount of governmental regulation of unrestrained private business enterprise — an increasing amount of what is called "social reform" or "social legislation." Such legislation has been based on the assumption that it is the duty of government, not merely to protect life and property and maintain civil order, but to promote the general welfare by improving the conditions of life for the less fortunate classes at the expense if necessary of the more fortunate classes. It is the form of collectivism which I have called "Social Democracy." The results attained have been attained by the democratic method, by correcting specific evils as they appear by specific measures which the people will support. This is the slow way, the hard way of achieving Social Democracy.

There are those who have maintained, and now maintain, that it is the futile way — the way that is doomed to failure. Other ways have, accordingly, been proposed and tried — the forms of collectivism which I have called Socialism, Communism, and Fascism. Let us take a look at them.

2

The theory of Communism is at least as old as Plato (fifth century B.C.) ; but in its modern form it was worked out by Karl Marx during the middle of the nineteenth century. Marxian Communism, or "scientific" Socialism (both words were used at that time) was based on a few simple ideas. The fundamental idea was that the course of historical development is inevitably determined by economic forces rather than by men's ideas about what ought to happen. The organization of society at any time, and men's ideas about it, are fundamentally determined by the most important form of wealth ("factors of production") . The class which controls this form of wealth is, by virtue of its economic power, the ruling class, and will remain such as long as the form of wealth which it controls remains the most important form of wealth; and the form of government, the prevailing customs and ideas, are such as are best suited to maintain the ruling class in power. But when another form of wealth becomes the most important basis of economic power, the class which controls this new form of wealth will inevitably dispossess the old ruling class, and new institutions, customs, and ideas will be established because they are better suited to maintain the economic power of the new ruling class. Such a transfer of economic power and change of institutions and ideas constitute what Marx called a social revolution. The efficient cause of the revolution is the transfer of economic power from one class to another; the new ideas and institutions are merely the necessary consequence of such a transfer of power. In short, the efficient cause of historical development, of "progress," is a persistent and inevitable "economic class conflict."

The liberal-democratic revolution of the eighteenth and nineteenth centuries, according to this philosophy, was the result of such an economic class conflict. It occurred because a new form of wealth ("capital") had come to be more important than the old form (land). The "capitalist class" which controlled the new form of wealth then dispossessed the old ruling class (landowning nobles), and the monarchical and feudal institutions and ideas that had maintained the landowning aristocracy in power were replaced by liberal-democratic institutions and ideas because they were better suited to maintain the power of the new ruling class of business men and bankers and lawyers. The new "freedoms" — representative government, freedom of speech and the press and religion, and freedom of competitive economic enterprise — were freedoms for the bourgeois capitalist class only. For the industrial laborers, the "proletariat," they were not freedoms at all, but merely devices for keeping them in subjection. Therefore, according to Marx, there necessarily developed within the capitalist system a new economic class conflict between the ruling class and the proletariat, and this class conflict would inevitably result in another social revolution.

The coming revolution would be inevitable, Marx

thought, because the capitalist system contained "contradictions" that would necessarily destroy it. The basic principle of the system was unrestrained competition for private profit. Such competition would enable the more intelligent and unscrupulous "capitalists" to drive the others out of business. Wealth would therefore be increasingly concentrated in the hands of a few, and the mass of the people would be reduced to the level of "wage slaves" earning a bare subsistence. But with the mass of the people impoverished, the market for goods would decline, industry would "contract," and sooner or later a series of increasingly disastrous business "crises" would end in the complete collapse of the capitalist system.

This would provide the necessary conditions for the social revolution, which would begin in the most highly industrialized country and spread to all the others. The revolution would be carried through, Marx seemed to think, by a spontaneous uprising of the people and the creation of a "Dictatorship of the Proletariat." Private property in land and industry would be abolished, the capitalist class would be liquidated, and the production and distribution of wealth would be directed by the government. With the revolution accomplished, the dictatorship would give way to a truly democratic government of the people. Since there would be no private property or competition for private profit, there would no longer be any "economic classes," and hence no "class conflict." The revolution would thus, according to Marx, be the end of the old world of oppression and the beginning of a new and better world of equality and justice, in which men would compete, not for private profit, but on the higher humane level of intellectual achievement and social service.

The Marxian philosophy of history and social evolution provided the workers of Europe with a kind of religion, a fighting faith. It assured them that their present oppression was a necessary part of the nature of things, but that the nature of things was on their side and would inevitably bring for them or for their children a world purged of all injustice. Their part was to understand the law of history, and while waiting for the coming revolution to prepare for it by uniting with their brothers in all countries for promoting the class conflict against the capitalists in all countries. This the industrial workers did by organizing Socialist societies and Socialist political parties in virtually all European countries. They adopted programs of "social reform" designed to benefit the workers in particular and the poor people in general, and elected deputies to the legislatures pledged to work for these measures. Such measures, however, were at first regarded as mere temporary expedients — crumbs which could be picked up from the capitalist table pending the coming of the revolution which would end the capitalist banquet once and for all.

But then, towards the end of the nineteenth century, faith in the Marxian doctrine of revolution declined. For one thing, the revolution seemed a long time in coming — much longer than Marx had thought. So far from impoverishing the mass of the people, the capitalist system seemed to be enriching them. Measures of "social reform" were doing a good deal to improve the conditions of the workers, and such measures were in part carried into effect by the

Socialist parties, which were able to elect more and more deputies to the legislatures. But the Socialist leaders found that the less they said about the coming revolution and the collapse of the capitalist system, the more votes they polled at the elections. Preaching the orthodox Marxian doctrine of violent revolution thus ceased to be good political tactics, and towards the end of the century the majority of the followers of Marx "revised" the orthodox Marxian doctrine. According to the "revised" doctrine, the revolution would come "gradually," by the legal democratic procedure. The great object still was the nationalization of land and industry, and the state control of the production and distribution of wealth; but this object would not necessarily be achieved by revolutionary violence and social upheaval.

Meantime the minority Socialist parties in most countries retained their faith in the orthodox Marxian doctrine of revolution by violence; and after the last war they generally took the name of "Communist" to distinguish their brand of Marxism from the "Socialist" or "revisionist" brand accepted by the majority parties. In Russia the majority (Bolsheviki) party came to be directed, after the last war, by Nicolai Lenin. Lenin accepted the basic ideas of Marx, but he disagreed with Marx in respect to the methods by which the revolution could be carried out. He realized that the mass of the people in Russia knew nothing about the philosophy of Marx, and cared less. He was therefore convinced that a revolution could never be carried through to a definite end by any spontaneous uprising of the people. It would have to be carried through by a small, highly disciplined party, composed of tried and reliable persons who accepted the Communist faith with a religious conviction and zeal. The revolution, to be successful, would have to be strictly planned, begun only when the circumstances were favorable, and carried through by a "dictatorship of the Communist Party" *for* the proletariat and probably in opposition to strong and persistent resistance of the mass of the people whom the revolution was designed to benefit.

Acting on this plan, Lenin and the Communist Party carried through the Russian Revolution of October 1917. The event would have surprised and disconcerted Karl Marx, who confidently expected the revolution to begin in the most highly industrialized country as a result of the collapse of the capitalist system. But Russia was one of the least highly industrialized countries of Europe, one in which the capitalist system, so far from being in a state of collapse, was not even well established. The Russian Revolution was the result of two circumstances, in the nature of historical "accidents," which neither the Marxian nor any other philosophy of history could have foreseen. One of these was the sudden collapse of the czarist authority as a result of the war: had it not been for the corruption and ineptitude of the czarist government in the last war, the czarist regime would have continued in power. The other circumstance was the presence and remarkable ability of Nicolai Lenin; apart from Lenin, it is safe to say, the revolution would not have resulted in the establishment of Communism.

Even so, the Russian Revolution turned out very differently from what Marx, or even Lenin himself, had hoped it would. After twenty-five years only one of the great basic ideals of Communism has been realized. This is the nationalization of land and industry, and the control and direction of the production and distribution of wealth by the government. Even this was accomplished only after fifteen years, in the face of bitter resistance by the peasant farmers, and only by systematic and merciless liquidation, not only of the capitalist class, but of the nonconforming proletariat itself. The "dictatorship," which Marx and Lenin thought would be only temporary, still exists under Joseph Stalin, more absolute even that it was under Lenin. In twenty-five years much has been accomplished. The country has been rapidly industrialized, the production of wealth has been greatly increased, and on the whole more equitably distributed than it was under the czarist regime. Illiteracy has been largely abolished, the standard of life for the majority of the people has been raised, and the majority of the people accept the system of government with loyalty and devotion. But the "classless" society which Marx predicted and Lenin hoped to establish has not yet emerged; and the "freedoms" which we think essential, and which Marx thought would be secured by the revolution (political freedom, freedom of speech and the press) do not as yet exist. History, and especially history in Russia, has almost completely refuted the Marxian philosophy of history.

No aspect of the Marxian philosophy of history has been more completely refuted by the course of historical events than the belief that the revolution would become an international revolution, wiping out national distinctions and dissolving the "bourgeois" sentiment of national patriotism. In Russia love of

"Mother Russia" proved stronger than the revolutionary ideal. In order to win the support of the Russian people Stalin had to appeal to the sentiment of nationalism and profound love of native soil which characterizes the Russian people; and today Russia, for all its Communism, is as strongly "nationalist" and as devoted to the "national interest" as any country in the world. There was another reason, however, for abandoning the ideal of international Communist revolution. It soon became obvious that there was no possibility of a Communist revolution in any other important country. Marx thought that a successful Communist revolution in one country would greatly aid the revolution in other countries. But in fact the establishment of Communism in Russia, so far from aiding the Communist revolution in other countries, really weakened it: the Revolution in Russia created a profound fear of Communism in all other countries, and thereby aided another sort of collectivist revolution. This other sort of collectivist revolution occurred first in Italy, where it took the name of Fascism, and then in Germany where it took the name of Nazism.

Fascism is the general term used to designate the form of government and social organization established in Italy by Mussolini, in Germany by Hitler, in Spain by Franco, and in other countries by leaders who imitated Mussolini or Hitler. The system varies a good deal in the different countries in which it has appeared, but all forms have certain common characteristics which make it one thing. In certain respects Fascism as established in Italy and Germany resembles Communism as established in Russia. Under both systems the government is a one-man and a one-party dictatorship. In both systems the liberties of the individual as they prevail in democratic countries are suppressed. And in both systems the government controls more or less completely the economic enterprises of the country.

But in other respects Fascism is radically different from Communism. Communism rests on a reasoned philosophy of history and politics which was systematically propagated for fifty years before it was realized in the Russian soviet system. In theory Communism is democratic — that is, the dictatorship is regarded as temporary, a necessary device for carrying through the revolution, to be replaced, as soon as the revolution is accomplished, by a government of, by, and for the people. In theory Communism is international — that is, it preaches the brotherhood of man and the equality of nations. In theory Communism is pro-intellectual — that is, it asserts that social organization and progress must be based on knowledge, and that knowledge can be acquired only by the free and disinterested search for truth. The Russian Soviet regime is not as yet a government by the people, although it professes to be a government of and for the people; it still exerts a pretty strict control of speech and the press and of teaching and learning. But the theory on which any system of politics is based is of vast importance, and it is possible, and indeed likely, that in time the Soviet government will become more democratic and the liberties of the individual less restricted.

In all of these respects Fascism is the opposite of Communism. Fascism is anti-democratic — the dictatorship and the suppression of individual liberties are permanent. It is anti-international — it denies the equality of races and nations as well as the equality of individuals. It is anti-intellectual — it regards science and the search for truth as of no importance except in so far as they can be used for the attainment of immediate political ends. Fascism suppresses the truth and practices brutality, not merely as a temporary device for ends that cannot for the moment be otherwise attained, but as permanent means inseparable from ultimate ends and possessing in themselves similar virtues. Communism was in no small degree an effect of the theory; but the theory of Fascism, if you can call it a theory, was in no sense a cause, but merely an effect of the thing itself. In origin the theory of Fascism was scarcely more than an invention of Mussolini to justify his personal ambition and fortify his personal power.

Mussolini started out as a Socialist who was opposed to Italy's entering the war of 1914. Then he changed his views and supported the war. At the close of the war Italy was on the verge of economic and political anarchy. All classes of people were disillusioned and dissatisfied with Italy's performance in the war and with her gains at the peace conference; and most people had lost all faith in the existing government, which was incredibly corrupt and inefficient. Mussolini exploited this situation. He organized a society composed of ex-Socialists and demobilized soldiers, which he called *Fascio di Combattimento* (Union of Combat). The society advocated many social reforms, such as heavy taxation of the rich; but its principal object was to combat Russian Communism. Bands of young men, wearing black shirts and armed with guns and clubs, were encouraged to beat up Communists, break up Communist meetings, and destroy Communist printing presses, literature, and red flags. Of course anyone whom they disliked for any reason, such as Socialists and Jews, were treated as Communists whether they were so or not.

These unlicensed and illegal acts made Mussolini popular with those who feared all forms of radicalism such as Socialism and Communism. Young men from all over Italy rushed to join the Fascist society; and as the society increased in numbers, Mussolini adopted every sort of idea that might increase his following. He appealed to the powerful business interests by denouncing strikes; to the great landowners by denouncing peasant uprisings; to the industrial workers by preaching the dignity of labor and the right to work; to small shopkeepers, lawyers, doctors, clerks, and school teachers by advocating the need of "discipline" and "order"; and to all classes by denouncing the government for having, by its feeble foreign policy, "betrayed the national honor." Mussolini was all things to all men; and he rose to power by convincing all classes that a strong government which suppressed many "liberties" would be better than a free government which was incapable of effective action of any sort. The theory by which Mussolini justified his activities and his power was expressed by the word "Fascism," which he derived from the Latin word *"fasces,"* meaning a bundle of rods carried by ancient Roman lictors as a symbol of political unity, authority, and punishment. According to Mussolini, unity, authority, and punishment had been destroyed by the democratic "liberties," which were no more than a license of the individual to do what he pleased. Fascism would restore order by giving all authority and power to a single leader who would thus represent, neither individuals nor classes nor parties, but the united will of the nation.

Italian Fascism was never profoundly dangerous because it was never profoundly serious — never more than a half-hearted belief that Mussolini would at least be better than the government he replaced. Mussolini himself was an educated, realistic, and skeptical man. He was neither sincere nor honest. He did not really believe in anything, not even the truth of the ideas he professed or the genuineness of his own bombast. But he was a superb actor, capable of simulating passion and conviction; and he appealed to the Italian's love of the dramatic, even if it was nothing more than melodramatic. It is said that on one occasion, when he was making a speech and had just delivered himself of a fine bit of rhetoric, Mussolini leaned over and whispered to Ciano: "Is that hot enough for them, or shall I make it hotter?" Then he straightened up, jutted out his chin, and made it hotter. The hotter it was, the more enthusiastically the audience took its cue and roared: "Duce, Duce, Duce!" But the audience, almost as well as Mussolini, knew it for what it was — political melodrama enlivened by a touch of the comic.

Italian Fascism was evil enough, as any system based on lies and brutality is evil; but compared with German Nazism it was essentially superficial. There was never anything comic about German Fascism. It also was based on lies and brutality; but Hitler believed his lies with the fanatical conviction and practiced his brutalities with the profound satisfaction that inspires the paranoid. He is an ignorant, frustrated, egocentric man, devoid of imagination, totally incapable of sympathy or pity, totally incapable of understanding any feeling or need but his own. He therefore represented best, not the intelligent and the cultivated, not even the ignorant, lowly people of good will, but the ignorant, frustrated people of ill will. He did not need to consider what these people would think or do. Since he was one of them, he represented them by just being himself, by doing in their name, and encouraging them to do on their own account, what gave him and would give them the highest sense of power and importance. Hitler was the ideal leader of the weak and the frustrated — those who as individuals have neither the brains nor the character to achieve anything, but united in mobs acquire a sense of success by imposing on superior people the humiliations which they themselves have experienced. Goering and Goebbels resemble Mussolini: they are the intelligent, realistic, and skeptical leaders of German Fascism who know what they are doing and know that it is a game. But Hitler and Himmler are the real, the dangerous leaders because, being themselves inherently vicious and brutal, they represent and are capable of releasing in the submerged and frustrated masses the vicious and brutal instincts that are inhibited by the customs and rules of civilized society. Hitler rose to power by the same tactics as those employed by Mussolini and by applying them to a similar condition of national disintegration; but German Fascism is far more dangerous than Italian Fascism because it is far more sincere in its fanaticism, and far more systematic and thoroughgoing in its denial of the elemental principles of truth, justice, and humanity.

Fascism is more dangerous than Communism, not only because it is a more complete denial of the principles of truth, justice, and humanity, but also because it is more flexible and therefore more readily adaptable to the historic traditions and national temperament of any country. It rests upon a few easily understood ideas: First, that the particular nation or race is superior to all others. Second, that the people of the superior race or nation derive from that superiority the right to do whatever they want to do without regard to the rights of inferior nations or races. Third, that the will of the superior race or nation is embodied in a Leader, to whom all individuals owe unquestioned obedience because he will enable the superior race or nation to realize its superiority. And fourth, that the superiority of the particular race or nation justifies its Leader in whatever distortion of truth and whatever application of force may be necessary to suppress all opposition to his and the nation's will. These ideas, being merely the expression of the sentiment of nationalism in its extreme form, are native in every country. They need no organized propaganda to spread them in any country which is disintegrated by widespread economic insecurity, class conflicts, and loss of of faith in the efficiency of the existing form of government. Under such circumstances they will appeal to ignorant and defeated men, to cynical and disillusioned men, to corrupt men on the make, and to all who are convinced that political authority is more essential than political liberty. All that is then needed is the right Leader.

The ideal Leader for a Fascist system had been admirably described by Harold Laski, no doubt with Hitler more especially in mind:[1]

> The leader must be immensely above his followers, but he must be also one with them and of them; distance must not interfere with the sense of intimate communion. So that leader, who is godlike, is also of common clay. He is the little man who failed in the "pluto-democracy" he came to supplant, so that all the little men who failed under that social order may recognize themselves in him.

Any country can produce such a man, and when the circumstances are favorable the people do not need to be carefully indoctrinated in an elaborate philosophy of history of foreign origin, or in any philosophy at all, to accept and follow him. They will accept and follow him because they recognize instinctively that he is one of them and with them, one who therefore knows what they feel and what they want. The Leader needs no philosophy. He does not need the terms "Fascism" or "Nazism." He will, if he is wise, choose a term that is native and familiar and in good odor. All that he needs to do is to apply the principle of direct action by methods of procedure that are familiar and acceptable to the people. Fascism is the most dangerous because the most insidious enemy of democracy. It does not require a violent revolution. It can come gradually, by imperceptible modification of existing institutions, and entrench itself under the forms of democracy before the people know that democracy has been destroyed.

[1] *Reflections on the Revolution of Our Time,* p. 129.

3

These are the four forms of collectivism that have
been proposed or tried in our time. They are alike in
one respect only: they all reflect the trend, inevitable
in our complex technological societies, towards an
increasing amount of governmental regulation of private economic enterprise. But they differ, often radically, in other and more important respects. They differ either in respect to the amount of governmental
regulation which is thought necessary, or in respect to
the means which are proposed for effecting the end
desired.

To make this difference vivid, let us represent the
four forms of collectivism (Social Democracy, Socialism, Communism, Fascism) by four outstanding persons: Franklin Roosevelt, Norman Thomas, Joseph
Stalin, and Adolf Hitler. Franklin Roosevelt is a social
democrat. He wishes to keep as much of the capitalist
system and of competition for private profit as possible, but believes that a good deal of governmental
regulation of private enterprise is necessary in order
to achieve the maximum production and an equitable
distribution of wealth; and he is entirely convinced
that whatever regulation is necessary should and can
be accomplished by the established democratic political procedure, and without surrendering any of our
democratic liberties.

Norman Thomas is a Socialist, in the strict party
sense of that term. He differs from Roosevelt in regard
to the capitalist system of private property and competition for private profit. These he regards as the
fundamental evil which must be abolished before

there can be a maximum production or any tolerably equitable distribution of wealth. He therefore believes it is necessary for the government to own and operate the great productive enterprises, as it now controls and operates the postal service. But in respect to the means by which this can and should be accomplished he agrees with Roosevelt. He does not believe, as the Communists do, that any violent revolution is either necessary or desirable. On the contrary, he believes that the desired end can and will be accomplished as soon as a majority of the people are convinced that it is necessary, by supporting the Socialist Party and its program and passing the necessary legislation by the established democratic procedure. Thus Roosevelt (social democrat) and Norman Thomas (Socialist) disagree as to the amount of governmental regulation that is necessary, but agree that whatever amount is necessary can be brought about by the peaceful democratic method.

Joseph Stalin is a Communist. He agrees with Norman Thomas that private property in land and industry and competition for private profit is the fundamental evil which must be abolished before there can be a government for all of the people rather than for the privileged capitalist class. But he does not believe that the capitalist system of private property can be abolished in any democratic country by democratic political methods. It can be accomplished only by a revolution, because the very class which needs to be dispossessed is the class that controls the government and shapes legislation in the capitalist democratic countries. The desired end can therefore be accomplished only by a revolutionary dictatorship, the temporary suppression of the democratic liberties, and the forcible "liquidation" of the capitalist class.

Adolf Hitler is a Fascist. Fascism need not have all the revolting characteristics of German Fascism. But wherever Fascism has been established it has abolished the democratic liberties and political procedure, established a dictatorship, and without technically abolishing private property in land and industry has subjected it to such complete governmental control that it amounts to the same thing. Thus Fascism and Communism agree in asking us to give up all three of the democratic liberties — private economic enterprise, freedom of speech and the press, and self-government. Socialism asks us to give up only one — private economic enterprise. Social Democracy does not ask us to give up any of the democratic liberties, but only to submit to whatever restrictions of private economic enterprise may be necessary for the economic welfare and security of the people as a whole.

Which of these four forms of collectivism do we want? It is useless to say that we do not want any of them. These are the four forms which the history of technological society in our time imposes. We must accept one of them. If this is so, then it need scarcely be said that the overwhelming majority of the people of the United States would not choose to have either Fascism or Communism. Almost as little would they choose to have Socialism. But it decidedly does need to be said that if they let things drift, if they do not give far more serious and intelligent attention to the task of achieving Social Democracy by the democratic method than they have as yet done, they will be in grave danger of getting one of the forms of collectivism which they least want to have. They cannot drift into Social Democracy. They cannot very easily drift into Communism or Socialism. If they let things drift the thing they are most likely to drift into is Fascism. The choice which we actually have is, then, I think, the choice between being intelligent enough to devise some method of making the capitalist system of private enterprise work and thereby preserving our democratic liberties, or of muddling along, playing politics, and ending up with some American brand of Fascism and the loss of our democratic liberties.

One reason why some brand of Fascism "can happen here" more easily than any brand of Communism is that we fear it less. This is indeed a curious and an interesting fact. Although we are fighting a desperate war to destroy Fascism in Germany, although it is everywhere proclaimed that German Fascism is the most evil thing now in the world and the chief menace to our democratic liberties, although we are allied with the Russian Communists in the effort to destroy German Fascism, and although Communism has made no conquests in the last twenty-five years, whereas Fascism has spread in many countries — in spite of all this the people of this country fear Communism more than they fear Fascism. Evidence of this is to be found in the popular support given to the fantastic "anti-Communist" investigations of the Dies Committee; in the fact that the easiest way to discredit any person or idea is to denounce the person or the idea as "Communist" or "Red," in the fact that government agents inquiring into the loyalty of persons seeking government war jobs ask such infantile questions as whether the person has ever been active in the support of labor unions, or given money to help the Spanish Loyalists, or subscribes to the *Nation* or the *New Republic,* or has many friends among the Jews. No doubt the explanation of this widespread fear of Communism is that for the last fifty years all radical political ideas have been identified, in the mind of the average American, with the words "communism" and "socialism." For the average American the two words mean the same thing. Other words even more commonly used are "Bolshevik" and "Red." These are the popular symbols of all that is politically radical, foreign, un-American, and therefore dangerous. Fascism is foreign too, but it is recent, and it is not as yet a symbol for a "doctrine" that can be insidiously propagated under cover. It is just a form of government associated with Hitler and Germany, Mussolini and Italy. The average American has been told, and may readily agree, that German Fascism is worse than Russian Communism. But why worry? We are fighting to destroy, and will destroy, German Fascism. And since we will surely destroy it, it obviously "can't happen here." This is why loyal and intelligent liberals like Robert Morse Lovett and William E. Dodd, Jr., are regarded as more dangerous to our American liberties than the Silver Shirts or the Chicago *Tribune.*

I do not think that Fascism will happen here, but it is foolish to say that it can't happen here, and it has a far better chance than Communism of happening here. The conditions that would make it possible would be another Great Depression more disastrous and more prolonged than the last one: general business stagnation for want of markets; twenty million people without jobs and without hope for the future;

farmers everywhere facing mortgage foreclosures, with crops rotting on the ground and no remedy in sight except to cut down the production of foodstuffs; labor unions discredited by gangster tactics, and business men in a mood to "smash the unions" at all costs; class conflicts too embittered to be reconciled and power politics too unrestrained to be joked about; a "bundles for Congress" movement sweeping the country — in short, economic disintegration and loss of faith in the slow, cumbersome, and expensive democratic political procedure. Such conditions might very easily bring to life the deep-seated, grim conviction of the average American that injustice and confusion are not things to be taken lying down, and release his impulse and capacity for "direct action" — the impulse and capacity that produced the "vigilance committees" on the frontier, the Ku-Klux Klan after the Civil War, and the concerted and effective off-the-record activities that defeated the prohibition amendment to the Constitution. A leader or leaders would of course be necessary, and forthcoming — a leader or leaders with the dynamic personality of a Theodore Roosevelt, the homespun ideas and hypnotic voice of a William Jennings Bryan, and the intellectual ingenuity of a Huey Long. The result, whatever form it might take, would not be called Fascism, still less Nazism; it would be heralded by some native American slogan, such as the "national clean-up," the "new Americanism," "efficiency for freedom," or more likely some as yet uncoined phrase even more relevant and expressive. And whatever form it might take, it would still be the American way of life.

I do not think this will happen here, but if we would

avoid the conditions which might, if unchecked, lead to it, we must after the war is over give at least as much intelligent attention to the old problem of achieving Social Democracy as we are now giving to the winning of the war. It is being said that the New Deal has been "scrapped." It would be truer to say that the pre-war New Deal has been absorbed by the wartime New Deal. The pre-war New Deal was a continuation of what Woodrow Wilson called the New Freedom, and what Theodore Roosevelt called the Square Deal. It was an attempt to solve what is called the "social problem," or what the Atlantic Charter refers to as "improved labor standards, economic adjustment and social security." What is needed for the solution of this social problem is easily stated: we need to have our industrial and agricultural enterprises working at full capacity producing the goods that are needed, and full employment of all the people at good wages so that the goods produced can be bought by the people that need or want them. How to bring about this result is far less easy to determine. The pre-war New Deal was an experiment — an effort to devise means of bringing it about which accomplished something, but not enough. Then the war came and forced us to adopt a wartime New Deal which makes the pre-war New Deal governmental intervention in business look like small potatoes, and which has very nearly attained the desired end of putting our industrial plants to work at full time and providing full employment for all the people.

The wartime New Deal has succeeded better than the pre-war New Deal for a variety of reasons. For two reasons more especially: first, because we know definitely what we have to do, which is to win the war; and second, because we are pretty thoroughly united in the desire and the determination to win it. But in order to fight and win the war it has been necessary, and generally recognized as necessary, to place in the hands of the government far more power than it has ever had in peacetime to regulate and co-ordinate the economic life of the country. The government has become a super-business enterprise, an over-all holding company, which determines what goods shall be produced and in what quantity, what men shall be employed by it in the armed services and government war jobs and what men must be "deferred" or reserved for war industries. All this calls for unlimited government spending, which means an unprecedented demand for goods and labor. According to Stuart Chase, the government was in June 1943 spending about eight billion dollars a month for goods and services. And it is for this reason that our industrial plants are now running at nearly full capacity, that unemployment has disappeared, and that the great majority of the people have much more money ("purchasing power") to buy what they need or want than they have had for a long time. The wartime New Deal is merely an extension of the pre-war New Deal — a more comprehensive and systematically planned intervention of government in the business enterprise and the economic life of the country.

But it will be said, and indeed is being said, that the war is a temporary emergency during which the government necessarily takes over, and when the emergency is ended the government ought to "stop meddling in business and let private business take over again"; government spending on the present mad scale must come to an end, and the "bureaucrats and college professors" down in Washington must stop messing things up and go home. So it is being said. But what would happen if on demobilization day the government stopped meddling in business, if overnight it stopped spending eight billion dollars a month and all the bureaucrats and college professors cleared up their desks and went home? The first thing that would happen is that forty-five million men now working directly or indirectly for the government would be out of a job, and a good proportion of them, including a good proportion of the twelve million soldiers, sailors, and airmen, would soon be on the street. And in no long time there would be an economic collapse which would make the Great Depression of 1929–33 look, by comparison, like a time of plenty and contentment.

When the war is over the government will necessarily cease to do many things which it is now doing, and no doubt it will cease to spend as much money. But there will still be an emergency, although of a different kind. There will be a demobilization emergency — the temporary emergency created by the necessity of getting back from a wartime to a peacetime economy. This will last for some time, and then will fade out into the old, familiar, permanent, and more difficult peacetime emergency which existed before the war began, and which the pre-war New Deal was an attempt to meet. To suppose that the peacetime emergency will be any less important or less insistent or less difficult than the wartime emergency, to suppose that the government will be able to by-pass this emergency and rely upon "business as usual" to maintain full production and full employment, is to be incredibly naïve and incapable of learning anything from the experience of the last fifty years.

Whatever party is in power after the war will find that the government cannot cease spending or cease meddling. It might conceivably cease muddling. It will at all events be confronted with the same problem which the pre-war New Deal was an attempt to solve. But the pre-war New Deal was not enough for the situation before the war, and will be even less so for the situation after the war is over. It was an experiment from which, however, we can learn much. The wartime New Deal is another experiment from which we should learn still more. And it is to be hoped that, learning much from these experiments, the demobilization emergency will prepare the way for a postwar New Deal which will avoid the most obvious defects of all previous new deals.

The chief defect of all our peacetime new deals, from Theodore to Franklin Roosevelt, is that they were all concerned primarily with particular measures designed to cure specific evils. When the banks were all on the verge of failure they were closed for a few days to tide them over. When millions of men were unemployed they were given temporary relief, or else jobs were rigged up to provide work for them. When farmers were desperate, mortgage foreclosures were forbidden temporarily, and in order to raise prices of farm products the raising of cotton and corn was restricted or the government bought the surplus and held it. And so on. But no adequate attempt was made to get at the underlying causes of the general collapse, and as a consequence there was no clear or agreed-upon idea of the ultimate end to be achieved. The chief defect of the pre-war New Deal was that it was too much concerned with curing particular evils and too little concerned with achieving some positive general good. It is an arresting and significant fact that the pre-war New Deal failed to abolish unemployment although that was its main object, whereas the wartime New Deal has virtually abolished unemployment although its main object was something else. The general object of the wartime New Deal is to win the war: the disappearance of unemployment is an incidental result of pursuing that general object. If I were Gilbert Chesterton I might say that the pre-war New Deal failed to cure unemployment because it tried to cure it, whereas the wartime New Deal succeeded in curing unemployment because it didn't try to.

This is something more than an amusing paradox. It means that if we could have a well-considered plan for promoting the national welfare — that is to say, for improving the standard of living for all the people — and were as united and determined in carrying it through as we are in winning the war, we could forget about business stagnation and unemployment. These evils would disappear as they have disappeared during the war; and their disappearance would be an incidental result of the effort to achieve a more positive and a more general object. Unfortunately, any nation is more easily united by the fear of an immediate and clearly discerned disaster than it is by the prospect of a debatable and uncertain future good. This is why it is easier to win the war than it will be to win the peace — that is to say, to solve the social problem. But at least a good starting-point for solving the social problem is to ask what specific things need to be done to raise the standard of living for all the people, and would be done if we were as united and militant for achieving that object as we are for winning the war.

Any comprehensive plan for raising the standard of living for all the people would obviously be concerned with such matters as sufficient food, clothing, shelter; adequate medical service; improved educational facilities, for vocational and professional training and for scientific research; extended facilities for recreation and amusement; disability and old-age insurance. What would this mean specifically? It would mean an enormous expansion in the production of food, clothes, houses, and all consumers' goods. It would mean a nation-state housing program, the abolition of slums, and the rebuilding of parts of a hundred or more cities to adapt them to the present and future conditions of business and transportation. It would mean a nation-state program for expanding, co-ordinating, and improving the system of transportation — highways, railroads, waterways, airways, and pipe lines. It would mean a nation-state program for the expansion and improvement of schools, colleges, and universities, for the building of public parks, recreation centers, museums, and art galleries. It would mean a nation-state program for building, equipping, and staffing more and better hospitals, asylums for the mentally defective, and centers for medical research. It would mean at least this; but such a systematic program would be capable of indefinite expansion.

It is obvious that such a comprehensive program could not be carried through, or even planned, without federal and state co-operation, supervision, and assistance all along the line. It would obviously require a good deal of governmental regulation of private business enterprise. But in carrying it through, the guiding principle should be to make the greatest possible use of private business enterprise. No program for promoting the national welfare can succeed unless it wins the support of the people — business men, farmers, and laborers — and no program will win the support of the business interests if it appears to business men in the light of measures which are primarily designed to restrict private enterprise. Capitalist business enterprise thrives only on expansion; and such a program for promoting the national welfare could succeed, therefore, only if and in so far as the agricultural and industrial interests could be induced to regard it as providing an opportunity for industrial and agricultural expansion. Only by uniting the private-profit motive with the desire to promote the national welfare could such a comprehensive program be carried through, but if that could be done the evils of business stagnation and mass unemployment would cease to trouble us.

I do not underrate the obstacles to carrying through any such comprehensive program. The chief difficulty would be to convince the industrial and agricultural interests and their representatives in Congress that it would be to their interests to support such a program, and even if that could be done there would be the inevitable conflict between regions and groups to get what they each thought was coming to them, which would be something more than their fair share. There would be, in short, the inevitable "pressure politics," and behind the pressure politics competition for private profit. The fundamental question is whether in the capitalist system the private-profit motive can ever be sufficiently reconciled with the desire for the general welfare. Perhaps not. But, at all events, apart from some such program it is difficult to foresee any situation which will provide business enterprise an opportunity for adequate and indefinite expansion. Failing such opportunity for expansion, we shall no doubt be forced to return to the policies and limited successes of the pre-war New Deal — mistaking symptoms for causes, attempting to abolish business stagnation and unemployment by giving subsidies to business men and relief checks to the unemployed. The chief difference is likely to be that the subsidies will have to be larger and the relief checks more numerous.

Supposing, however, that such a comprehensive program or something like it could be carried through; supposing that we succeed by whatever means in having full production and full employment — what then? Then we should have surplus goods to be sold abroad, which could not be sold abroad, however, unless foreign countries were in a position to pay for them and were permitted to pay for them in goods exported to this country. Full production and full employment can be maintained in an undeveloped country like Russia where the capitalist system has been abolished and the economic life of the community is entirely controlled by government decree. But it is difficult to see how it can be done in the United States, or any other country under the capitalist system, if the rest of the world is impoverished. It certainly cannot be done in the United States if the

171

United States, as a chief creditor country, expects to sell goods and services abroad and at the same time erects a Hawley-Smoot tariff, which makes it impossible for foreign countries to pay by selling us their goods in exchange. If we return to that policy, or to anything like it, we shall only undermine our own export trade, alienate half the world, contribute to the collapse of world economy, and do our share to prepare the way for another global war.

It is as impossible for highly industrialized, capitalist countries to live in economic as in political isolation. The effort to make a new and better world at home is, therefore, inseparable in the long run from the making of a new and better world in international relations. This brings us to the question: What kind of new international order can we have?

7

What Kind of International Political Order Can We Have?

EVERYBODY, or at least everybody who writes books about it, seems to take it for granted that after the war is over we must have some kind of new international order, some kind of new and better world in international relations. And since the principal reason for the widespread interest in the question is the war and its multiplied disasters, the projects for a new international order are mostly concerned with the object of preventing war. The Atlantic Charter refers to the new international order as "a wider and permanent system of general security." This statement is about as broad and indefinite as any statement could be. It is so broad and indefinite that it would describe any and every sort of project, ranging from a mere military alliance of the victorious states, or some of them, to the most idealistic H. G. Wellsian dream of a super world-state establishing a reign of law and order and liberty for all mankind.

Most of the current projects for a new international order fall somewhere between these two extremes. The idea of an alliance between the victorious states (Great Britain, the United States, Russia, maybe China) is mostly rejected because it seems to be nothing new, but merely a modification of the old and discredited policy of a "balance of power." Such an alliance might prevent war as long as the allies held together, but only, it is feared, at the high cost of world domination by the more powerful at the expense of the less powerful countries. On the other hand, the idea of a super-world-state in which the independence of the several states would disappear, very much as the independence of the several states of our country has disappeared in the "more perfect union" under the Constitution, apparently seems to most people too grandiose, too much in the nature of wishful thinking, to be practicable. Most of the current projects therefore steer a middle course between these two extremes by proposing some sort of union, league, confederation, or federation of states, of European states perhaps, or of all states, in which the several states will retain more or less power of self-government, but will turn over to the league or federation more or less authority for settling international disputes and preventing war.

The makers of these projects for a new international order rarely use the word "league" to describe their projects, probably because the failure of the League of Nations has given the word a bad sound. The term commonly used is "federation," which by common usage implies something stronger than a league. The term "federation" commonly means a permanent union of states in which the several states turn over to a federal government the control of certain matters of common interest. The federal government may have much power or very little. Our own federal government, under the original Articles of Confederation,

174

had the power to make laws but no power to enforce them. Under the present Constitution the federal government has much broader powers, in respect both to making and to enforcing laws. A federation may thus be a "strong" or a "weak" federation; but a federation, in the usual sense of the term, must at least provide for a federal government with some power of making laws binding on the several states that compose it.

In this sense of the term some of the current projects for a new international order are federations only in name. They are in fact no more than proposals for reviving and strengthening the present defunct League of Nations. The idea seems to be that the old League failed because it had no military power to back up its decisions; and in these projects this weakness is remedied by providing for an "international police force." But other current projects, especially those that confine the federation to the states of Europe, are more properly called federations. They suggest the creation of a European federal government, with a federal legislature, federal courts, and a federal army. The basic idea of such projects seems to be that the European states can and should form a United States of Europe more or less on the model of such successful federations as that of Switzerland, the Dutch Netherlands, and more especially the United States of America.

What can be said for these two different projects for a new international order? It would certainly not be difficult to revive and strengthen the present defunct League of Nations by providing it with an "international police force" — whatever that may mean. But the relevant question is: Would that make it any more effective than it was without an internationel police force? A real federation of Europe, on the model of the United States, would no doubt be effective. But the relevant question is: Could such a federation be created under the conditions that will certainly prevail after the war is ended? In considering the kind of new international order we can have, much depends on the answers we give to these two questions.

1

The League of Nations was not an invention of Woodrow Wilson. Since the seventeenth century, to go no farther back, many projects of a similar nature have been proposed. The best-known project in the seventeenth century was Sully's so-called *Grand Design of Henry IV;* in the eighteenth century, the Abbé Saint-Pierre's *Project for Making Peace Perpetual in Europe.* In the nineteenth century similar projects were supported by the organized peace societies, and repeatedly recommended to the governments of Europe by the international peace congresses. All of these projects, including Woodrow Wilson's League of Nations, although differing in detail, were essentially alike in their purposes and in the means proposed for attaining the end desired.

The argument which supports them runs somewhat as follows: War is admittedly a major evil which all states have an interest in abolishing. But no one state can renounce war unless the others also renounce it. Therefore, let all the states of Europe, or of the world, bind themselves, in a solemn treaty, constitution, or covenant, to do three things: First, to recognize the form of government and territorial limits, with such modifications as may be agreed upon in the treaty or covenant, of all the member states. Second, to establish an international tribunal or procedure for settling disputes between two or more states which the states concerned cannot settle themselves by peaceful means. Third, to apply such "sanctions" (diplomatic, economic, military) as are provided for in the treaty or covenant against any state or states that refuse to accept the decision of the tribunal. This argument is a sound one and any such league or federation would prevent war only on the condition that all the member states, or most of them, do what by signing the treaty or covenant they have promised to do. The fundamental assumption of all such leagues is that the member states will do what they have promised to do, and for the following reason: War is an evil of such magnitude that the prevention of any particular war must always be, for the great majority of states not directly involved in the dispute that leads to it, more important than any other interest which might dispose them to allow that particular war to occur.

On these assumptions and in accord with this procedure the League of Nations was created after the last war for the purpose of preventing future wars. But it failed completely to achieve that purpose. Why? Two reasons are commonly given for the failure of the League. One is that it had not at its disposal an "international police force" capable of backing up its decisions. The other is that the United States refused to join it. Let us examine these assertions.

Supposing the League had been provided with an international police force to back up its decisions.

How would this police force have been recruited? Where would it have been stationed? From what authority would it have taken orders? How large would it have had to be in order to arrest Mussolini in his conquest of Ethiopia, or to arrest the Japanese in their conquest of China, or to arrest Hitler in his conquest of Czechoslovakia, or to arrest Stalin in his war on Finland? I should suppose it would have been recruited from the member states in proportion to their military or other strength. I cannot imagine where it would have been stationed. It would have had to be, in the various crucial instances mentioned, stronger than the Italian, the Japanese, the German, the Russian army. Some police force, certainly! And to complete the picture, a considerable part of this police force would have had to take orders from the League to fight the very country from which it was recruited. The League failed, not for want of a police force to back its decisions, but because, in all the crucial situations, there were no decisions to be enforced. It failed because, being nothing but an agent of the member states, it could do only what the chief member states were willing to use it for doing; and in the crucial situations the member states were not willing to do what by signing the covenant they had promised to do. Since they were unwilling, no police force that could conceivably have been placed at the disposal of the League would have been sufficient to compel them; and if they had been willing, no police force at all would have been necessary.

But it is said that if the United States had only joined the League it would have been strong enough to prevent war — to prevent the present war. Maybe the present war might have been prevented if the United States had joined the League. But not because it joined the League; only because the United States, France, and Great Britain might have been sufficiently united, as a result of the United States' participation in European affairs, to act with promptness and decision to stop the aggressions of Hitler. An alliance of France, Great Britain, and the United States existed during the last war. It has had to be reconstructed again to conduct the present war. If it had been maintained and perfected after 1919 the present war might indeed have been prevented. Not, however, because these countries were in the League, but because their national interests disposed them, and their combined power enabled them, to prevent it. The presence of the United States in the League would not have prevented Germany, Italy, or Japan from withdrawing from the League when they decided that it no longer served their interests; and when these countries withdrew from the League it ceased to exist as a means of preventing war. If these states were bent on war nothing could prevent them but the resistance of other states that remained in the League. But in that case the League would have been only another name for a military alliance of one group of states against another.

The League of Nations failed in the last analysis, as any similar league will fail, for three reasons. One is that it was formed for too limited, too negative purposes. Existing primarily to prevent particular wars, it could act only when it was too late — when the disputes leading to the particular war were too fully matured to be settled by peaceful means. Another is that it was based on a false assumption. It is not true that the prevention of war is always a major national interest. Every state now engaged in the present war is engaged in it because it regards some things, such as national independence, as far more important than the prevention of war. The third reason is that it is impossible to transfer political power from the states that have it to a league of fifty or twenty theoretically equal but in fact very unequal states by treaties agreed to or covenants adopted, however solemnly. In spite of promises and good intentions, political power will remain where it is, chiefly in a few great states; and the issue of peace or war will depend, League or no League, upon the conflict of real or supposed national interests of these states and the inevitable "power politics" played by them, whether through the forms and procedure of the league or not.

To say that the League of Nations failed to prevent war is not to say that it failed altogether. The League was a useful experiment in international co-operation, and it accomplished much that was worth while in that way. But its successes were aside from its main purpose. As an international fact-finding agency it has provided much valuable information and has acted as an international clearing-house for dealing with many problems — notably in connection with labor conditions, traffic in narcotics and prostitution, and the financial rehabilitation of bankrupt states. Divested of its war-prevention apparatus, it might well be maintained for the sort of activity in which it has proved useful. It has been useful even for its failure to prevent war, since we can learn from its failure that any successful effort to create a new international order must be directed, not to the prevention of particular wars, but to the elimination of those underlying conditions that make wars inevitable.

If a league of nations or of states would not be effective for this purpose, what about a real federation? Since Europe seems to be the center from which world wars are generated, there are many people who advocate a real federation of European states — a United States of Europe on the model of the United States of America. It is pointed out that the thirteen original states forming the American union were or claimed to be independent sovereign states, and that if they had retained that independence the North American continent might have been as distracted as Europe has been by diplomatic intrigue and periodical wars for the maintenance or the readjustment of the balance of power. But this unhappy experience of Europe was avoided by the federation under the Constitution of 1787. The Constitution was not adopted for the sole negative purpose of preventing war, but for the positive political ends for which all states exist — one of these being to provide for the common defense, another to promote the general welfare. Thus the American federation, having been founded to deal with the day-by-day problems of peace, did all that any federation could do to prevent war. Why then, it is asked, could European wars not be prevented by creating a similar federal state designed to provide for the common defense and to promote the general welfare?

No doubt they could if it were possible to create a European federation on the model of the United States. But it has not hitherto been possible, and the reason is that the conditions in Europe have never been as favorable for such a federation as they were in

America in 1787. The people inhabiting the thirteen original states for a hundred years or more had been united under the British government. They were predominantly English in origin, and with few exceptions spoke the English language. They had all much the same local political and economic institutions, social customs, and ideas about morality and religion. During the Revolution they came to think of themselves as forming one nation. The Constitution of 1787 did not make the people of the thirteen colonies one nation. On the contrary, it was but the formal expression of a union already existing and easily cemented because the people included in it had all much the same needs and interests, and much the same ideas about how they could best be safeguarded and promoted. In short, the conditions for creating a United States of America were about as favorable as they well could be. But even so, it was necessary, seventy-three years after the Constitution was adopted, to fight a civil war to preserve the Union.

No such favorable conditions have ever existed in Europe, and never perhaps were they so little favorable as now. It is true that there is, or was, a "European civilization" which is quite distinct from the civilization, let us say, of China or India. This "European cvilization," in which all European countries share, was largely shaped in fundamentals by Greek thought, Roman political institutions, and the ethical and moral teachings of Christianity. But whereas in the United States the conditions have all been favorable to the creation of one nation, in Europe, since the thirteenth century, all the conditions have operated to create many nations. There are in Europe more than twenty distinct nations, differing in racial origin, language, social customs, national character, and in many cases animated by mutual rivalries and animosities deeply rooted in past experience and confirmed by repeated military conflicts and wars of conquest. When John Adams went to Philadelphia in 1774 to attend the first Continental Congress, he had never before been outside of New England, and it was with the eager curiosity of a tourist that he observed the people and the customs of New York and Pennsylvania. But the differences between the people of Massachusetts and New York, or of Pennsylvania and Virginia, were as nothing compared with the differences between French and Germans, Bulgarians and Serbians, Poles and Russians, Greeks and Albanians. The various peoples of Europe are not, and have never thought of themselves as being, one nation, nor have they ever desired to be united under one government, even a federal government with any power, even the slightest, to interfere with the governments to which they have mostly been long subject and to which they are mostly much attached. This is why it has never hitherto been possible, in spite of repeated and often futile wars, to create a United States of Europe on the model of the United States of America.

It is less possible at the present time than it ever was before. For ten years the Germans have accepted a political philosophy, and established political institutions, which the other nations of Europe regard as a denial and a destruction of all that they associate, or ever have associated, with European civilization. For five years past the Germans have done everything it was possible to do to bring upon themselves a universal and concentrated hatred such as no nation of Europe has ever before incurred. When the German armies first invaded Russia, the Russians made a distinction between "Nazis" and other Germans. Now they make no such distinction. The Russians now regard all Germans as Nazis — that is to say, a species of mad subhuman beast which it is a virtue to destroy without pity or remorse. This feeling is shared by the people of the conquered and devastated countries of Europe. Can anyone suppose that Russians, Poles, Czechs, Danes, Norwegians, Dutch, French, Greeks, Serbs, or even Italians will after the war, or within any foreseeable future, be in a mood to forgive and forget, or have the slightest desire to join in a European federation in which eighty million Germans would necessarily play a major role? It is unthinkable. An alliance of the European states against Germany, yes, that is possible and likely enough. But a United States of Europe with Germany excluded would be like a United States of America with the Middle West excluded. It would not be, at all events, what the advocates of European federation have in mind.

For these reasons I think we are justified in believing that a federation of Europe on the model of the United States could not be created, and that a league of nations on the model of the present one, with or without an international police force, would not be effective. There is, however, an additional point to be noted in connection with a league or a federation. It concerns disarmament. Woodrow Wilson's faith in the success of the League of Nations was founded in no small measure on the possibility of reducing "national armaments . . . to the lowest point consistent with domestic safety"; and a federation of Europe on the model of the United States, or any similar federation, would obviously require a similar reduction. But in 1919 the possibility of general disarmament by the victorious states was so slight that the subject was at no time seriously considered. And if anything is certain it is that a general disarmament will be even less possible after the present war than it was after the last one. This fact alone is sufficient to defeat whatever hopes may be placed on a league or a federation as the basis of a new international order.

For all that, it now seems likely that an attempt will be made to create some sort of league or federation to prevent war. But in any case there will first have to be a preliminary political settlement of Europe and the Far East; and the possibility of a new international order, league or no league, will depend in no small part on the nature and success of that political settlement — on the states, large and small, that emerge, on their several interests, and on the "balance of power" that is thereby established.

2

Mr. Herbert Hoover has suggested that the United Nations should authorize some of the more influential members to act for all of them, so to speak as "trustees," in making the preliminary settlement after the war is over. Whether the United Nations do this or not, the effect will be much the same. The term "United Nations" is a somewhat misleading one. Most of the United Nations are not engaged in the war at all; many of them are engaged in it only in so far as their subjection to Germany or Japan permits. So far as winning the war is concerned, Russia, China, the British Commonwealth of Nations, and the United States are now acting as "trustees" of the United Nations. When the war is ended they will in effect act as trustees in making the peace. That is to say, circumstances and their own power will impose upon them, with or without formal action by other states, the chief responsibility.

In the Far East the chief responsibility will fall to China, Great Britain, and the United States; in Europe, to Russia, Great Britain, and the United States. It now seems likely that the war against Germany will be won before the war against Japan is finished, in which case preliminary measures for peace in Europe will be in process of adoption while the war is still being conducted in the Far East. For this reason, and because Europe is the center of our industrialized, technological civilization, the prospect for any new and better international order depends very largely upon the wisdom displayed and the measures taken for replacing Hitler's "new order in Europe" with another and better one. Rarely in the history of the world, therefore, has greater responsibility fallen to any countries than will fall to the United States, Great Britain, and Russia at the end of the present war.

This is generally admitted. The world is waiting, so to speak, to see what these three countries will do to "win the peace" after they have won the war. Responsible leaders in all three countries have expressed the desire and the determination to establish a durable peace — "After the final destruction of the Nazi tyranny, they hope to see established a peace which will afford to all nations the means of dwelling in safety within their own boundaries." There is no reason to believe that any one of these countries is not entirely sincere in its desire to establish such a peace. But neither is there any reason to believe that any one of them, in making the peace, will not be guided primarily by what it regards as its essential national interest. Russia, Great Britain, and the United States are now firmly united by the primary and common need of defeating Germany. But there is no use blinking the fact that when Germany is defeated and helpless that bond of unity will be weakened, or that in making the peace other and perhaps divergent interests will come into play. The fundamental question, therefore, is whether the real or supposed national interests of Russia, Great Britain, and the United States will enable them to agree on the essential terms of a European settlement, or will bring them into irreconcilable conflict. What, then, are the interests that may serve to unite these countries, and what are the interests that may serve to separate them?

It is obvious that the United States and the British Commonwealth of Nations have more interests in common than either has with Russia. They are inhabited by people who speak the same language, share a common culture, are attached to essentially the same political ideas and institutions, and have the same conception of justice and fair dealing. But apart from all this Great Britain and the United States will necessarily regard the settlement of Europe from the point of view of a set of primary interests which Russia does not share. The primary interest of both Great Britain and the United States is the defense and security of what Walter Lippmann happily calls the "Atlantic Community." In the narrow and strict sense of "power politics" this means that both Great Britain and the United States have a primary interest in preventing any continental European state from acquiring naval or political ascendancy in the Atlantic Ocean or the countries that border upon it.

This primary interest has always shaped British policy. In the sixteenth century, when Spain was the dominant European and naval power, England fought to destroy that ascendancy in Europe and on the sea. In the seventeenth and eighteenth centuries, when France acquired ascendancy in Europe and aimed to acquire colonial and naval power, Great Britain fought against France, and made alliances with whatever European country (Austria or Prussia) happened for the time being to be opposed to France. In the twentieth century, when Germany became the most powerful state in Europe and threatened to become a first-class naval and colonial power, Great Britain made an alliance with France and became the enemy of Germany. Great Britain, as a highly industrialized country and the center of the British Commonwealth of Nations, must necessarily be a great naval power, and it is inevitable that she should be opposed to any continental European state which aims to dominate Europe and acquire naval ascendancy in the Atlantic.

This is also, and has been for more than a century, a primary interest of the United States. Those of us (and unfortunately there are many) who think that we are a nation of starry-eyed idealists who have been twice tricked by the British into a European war in order to "pull their chestnuts out of the fire" have read the history of their country to little purpose. The truth is rather that the existence and friendliness of the British Empire, and the power of the British fleet, have for more than a century enabled us to roast our own chestnuts at leisure and eat them in security. Thomas Jefferson, an anti-imperialist if there ever was one, and with less reason for liking the British than we have, had a firmer grasp of international political realities than some of his present disciples seem to have. When France acquired from Spain the provinces of Florida and the great territory west of the Mississippi known as Louisiana, he pushed through the purchase of Louisiana, in spite of the fact that he was assuming powers which he believed the Constitution did not give him. He was willing to assume these powers because he believed the measure to be of the greatest importance, and for the following reasons, stated in a letter to R. R. Livingston (April 18, 1802):

The cession of Louisiana and the Floridas works most sorely on the United States. . . . The day that France takes possession of N. Orleans . . . seals the union of the two nations that in conjunction can maintain exclusive possession of the [Atlantic] ocean. From that moment we must marry ourselves to the British fleet and nation. We must turn all our attentions to a maritime force, for which our resources place us on very high grounds; and having formed and cemented together a power which may render reinforcement of her settlements here impossible to France, make the first cannon, which shall be fired in Europe the signal for tearing up any settlement she may have made, and for holding the two continents of America in sequestration for the common purposes of the united British and American nations.

This is an admirable expression of the fact that history and geography make the United States and Great Britain natural allies against any European power that aims to acquire naval control of the Atlantic and political power in the two Americas. It was for this reason that in 1821 President Monroe proclaimed the famous Monroe Doctrine, declaring that any attempt of the continental European powers to extend their political system to the New World would be regarded as an unfriendly act. The responsibility involved in making this declaration was assumed, and could have been assumed, only because the United States had been assured that Great Britain would support it. From that time to this our first line of defense in the Atlantic has been the existence and friendliness of the British Empire and the power of the British navy. During the nineteenth century that fact was not apparent because no European power (except France in the abortive attempt to establish a Mexican empire) made any effort to extend its naval or political power in the Western Hemisphere. But when Germany adopted a policy of naval and colonial expansion the similarity of British and American interests soon became obvious; and during the last and the present war we have had to "marry ourselves to the British fleet and nation" for essentially the same reasons as those given by Jefferson in 1802. The crucial spot now is not New Orleans but the Panama Canal, and it is now not France that threatens but Germany. But the principle is the same. We entered both wars, not because we were tricked by the British into pulling their chestnuts out of the fire, but because we have the same primary interest that the British have in preventing any European power from acquiring naval control of the Atlantic and thus endangering the peace and safety of the Atlantic Community.

The present war has made this so obvious that it is incredible anyone should fail to see it. The present war has also made it obvious that in any war waged in Europe by Great Britain and the United States for the defense of the Atlantic Community France is the indispensable "bridgehead." When that bridgehead was lost in June 1940, England was threatened with invasion and conquest, and the way was open for Germany to take Gibraltar, Dakar, and the Azores Islands — points from which South America, the United States, and Canada could have been attacked. If the British Empire had collapsed, the chief burden of defending the Atlantic Community would have fallen to us; and in that case no one would have had to have it explained in words of one syllable that the existence of the British Empire and the British fleet is a major national interest of the United States. Even as it turned out, with France lost but British power intact, it was only with the greatest difficulty that Britain and the United States together were able to acquire, from Africa, the less desirable bridgehead of Sicily and Italy. When France is recovered as a bridgehead, the end of the war against Germany will be in sight. France is therefore an essential ally of Great Britain and the United States for the defense of the Atlantic Community; and with France should be included the smaller democracies of western Europe (Switzerland, Belgium, Holland, and the Scandinavian countries)

191

since their security depends on the security of France and Great Britain, and their political ideas and institutions are essentially the same.

3

In the European settlement Great Britain and the United States will thus be acting for themselves primarily, but also, as "trustees" if you like, for the Atlantic Community — for South America, Canada, France, and the smaller democracies of western Europe. For them the essentials of such a settlement will be naval ascendancy in the Atlantic, a strong France, the restoration of Belgium, Holland, and the conquered Scandinavian countries, the destruction of Nazi power and the establishment in Germany and Italy of governments that are democratic in some sense of the term, or at all events that bear no resemblance to the Fascist or Nazi systems. The question is, would such a settlement, thus stated in terms of its broad general purposes, run counter to the national interests of Russia?

There is no reason to suppose that it would. Russia is not directly interested in the Atlantic Community or the settlement of western Europe. The primary interest of Russia in the European settlement arises from the fact that her western frontier, from the Baltic to the Black Sea, brings her into intimate relations with Poland, Czechoslovakia, Hungary, the Balkan states, and Germany. In the region of border states east of Germany, Russia has a major interest which the countries of the Atlantic Community do not share. Stalin has already made this clear by stating that Russia will retain certain parts of Poland and certain other strategic territories taken by Russia in 1939. He has also stated that he will oppose the creation of any federation of the border and Balkan states under Polish leadership. Something like eighty per cent of the people of these border and Balkan countries are peasant farmers. They are on the whole bitterly hostile to the Fascist or semi-Fascist governments supported by the upper classes and too often maintained only by Quisling adventurers with German or Italian backing. They are strongly in favor of governments by and for the farmers — governments which, although not Communist, would not be hostile to Soviet Russia. Stalin will certainly be in favor of such governments, and will certainly be opposed to any attempt, on the part of Great Britain and the United States, to set up governments or federations of governments on the Russian frontier that are designed, or that seem to him to be designed, to serve as a European barrier against Russian influence or the spread of Russian political ideas. It would be unwise, and futile besides, for Great Britain and the United States to make any such attempt, or otherwise to antagonize Russia in the settlement of eastern Europe, where Russia has the major interest, has made the major sacrifices, and will in any case have the major power. Their role in the settlement of eastern Europe should be that of friendly mediators, of "good brokers," working disinterestedly for a settlement that will be satisfactory to Russia and at the same time as satisfactory to the border countries as the conflicting interests and aspirations of those countries permit.

But supposing that Russia, Great Britain, and the United States can agree on the settlement of eastern

Europe, what about Germany? Germany lies midway between Russia and the western powers. The settlement of Germany is the central problem in the entire European settlement; and in the settlement of Germany the Russian and the Atlantic communities have an equal and in both cases a major interest. Russia, Great Britain, and the United States are now united in the war to destroy Nazi Germany. Will they be able to remain united in the effort to reconstruct a non-Nazi Germany?

There should be no insuperable difficulties provided they can avoid mutual suspicion and distrust — provided they can regard the German settlement as a means of securing peace and order in Europe rather than as an instrument in the conflict between Russian Communism and Western "capitalist democracy." From the point of view of peace and order in Europe their interests have in general been the same. Great Britain and Russia have often been at odds in other parts of the world — in the Near East, in central Asia, in the Far East; but they have commonly been equally opposed to the domination of Europe by any continental state — France under Napoleon, Germany in the last and the present war. As for Russia and the United States, their relations have never been unfriendly. It is true that we do not like the Russian form of government, any more than the Russians like ours; and this "ideological" difference has for the most part always existed. But for all that, the national interests of the two countries have never brought them into conflict. On the contrary. During the American Revolution Russia maintained a friendly neutrality. In the Civil War Russia favored the North rather than the

South. And in both World Wars Russia and the United States were opposed to Germany.

We may assume, therefore, that Russia, Great Britain, and the United States will all desire a German settlement that will make it impossible for Germany within any near future to endanger European peace and security. But what specific means will they regard as essential to this end? On the following points I think it likely that they will be agreed. Germany must be completely defeated. Individual Nazis, principals or agents, responsible for manifest crimes against accepted rules of warfare or common decency, must be punished. Property in occupied countries unnecessarily destroyed or taken out of the country must be, so far as possible, restored or paid for. Germany must be confined to her former boundaries. Provision must be made for enabling the German people to choose freely the form of government they prefer, which will be recognized, provided it be not a Nazi system or anything resembling it, as soon as it gives evidence of stability and a disposition to assume in good faith the obligations imposed on Germany by the peace. On these points it seems likely that Russia, Great Britain, and the United States will be in agreement. But statements recently made in connection with the National Committee of Free Germany in Moscow seem to indicate a difference of opinion on certain important points. The chief difference seems to be that whereas Great Britain and the United States insist on "unconditional surrender" and complete disarmament, Russia might be satisfied with conditional surrender and not averse to the maintenance of a strong German army.

Too much may easily be made of these differences. It is difficult indeed to believe that Russians, who have had a long experience of German atrocities at their worst, can be in favor of any conditional surrender or of keeping a strong German army intact. It is quite possible that all of this is a propaganda maneuver on the part of Stalin, designed to hurry up what he regards as the too leisurely effort of the British and Americans to create a "second front." The only other plausible explanation is far more serious. It is that Stalin believes that a completely disarmed Germany, occupied and policed for a considerable period by British and American forces, would be a greater danger to Russia than a Germany defeated and no longer dangerous but still sufficiently armed and organized to serve as a counterweight against the united power of Britain and America. If this idea is in the mind of Stalin, no matter how it got there, and especially if it got and remains there because Great Britain and the United States think it necessary to disarm and police Germany as a safeguard against the extension of Russian power and Communist ideas in Europe — if that is and remains the situation, then the prospect for a durable peace through the co-operation of Russia, Great Britain, and the United States is remote indeed.[1]

If this mutual distrust and suspicion exists, and to a less extent even if it doesn't, the danger of a clash between Russia on the one side and Great Britain and the United States on the other is most likely to arise in connection with the form of government to be es-

---

[1] These differences appear to have been ironed out at the Moscow Conference, but it is possible that they might arise again after the war is over.

tablished in Germany. All three powers are in favor of a "free Germany," which seems to mean a form of government in some sense democratic and acceptable to the people. But Russia may have one idea as to what a democratic government is, and Great Britain and the United States may have another. This is especially likely to be the case if the German people are themselves sharply divided on the question. It is quite possible that when, with the establishment of order in Germany, political life revives, the country may be too sharply and evenly divided for them to choose freely any form of government "acceptable to the people." The division might very well take the form of an irreconcilable class conflict between the industrial and conservative groups favoring a conservative "capitalist democracy," and the working and dispossessed classes determined to have a radical "social democracy." In that case it is reasonable to suppose that Stalin would favor the "proletariat" against the "capitalists," and it is not at all impossible to suppose that Great Britain and the United States would favor the "capitalists" in the belief that any form of government favored by Stalin would give Russia an undue influence in Germany and open the way for the spread of Communism in central Europe. It seems reasonable to suppose this. But if we are to take the Russian support of the Free Germany Committee seriously, it looks as if Stalin might prefer a "conservative" German government after all. It would be ironical indeed if in making the German settlement Russia should be found valiantly defending "capitalist democracy" and Great Britain and the United States insisting on a genuine "government by the people."

197

But all this at the present writing (December, 1943) is no more than speculation. No one knows as yet, except the responsible leaders of the three countries concerned, whether any attempt was made at the Moscow Conference to reach an agreement on the essentials of the post-war settlement of Germany. It is at all events of the first importance that such an agreement should be reached before the war is won; for if Germany becomes a bone of contention between Russia on the one side and Great Britain and the United States on the other, the way is open for Germany to play one side against the other, and the only chance for creating a new international order will have been lost.

Assuming, however, that Russia, Great Britain, and the United States do not clash over the settlement of Germany and eastern Europe, no serious differences are likely to arise between them over the settlement of Italy, France, and the other countries of western Europe. If disputes over boundaries arise, they are not likely to be serious. The form of government to be established in Italy, in France and other conquered countries can be decided by the people concerned, none of which is at all likely to be in favor of any form of Fascism. In connection with Italy and France, however, the much debated question of "imperialism" will arise. It can be taken for granted that no part of her former African empire will be restored to Italy. But what about Tunisia, Algeria, and French Morocco? It is extremely unlikely that France will be willing to withdraw from these countries. If not, Great Britain will be in no position to insist upon it so long as she retains her African possessions. Nor will she, I should think, even desire it; and it is unlikely that either Russia or the United States will be willing to alienate both France and Great Britain in order to obtain for the people of North Africa the right of political self-determination. Besides, there is Spanish Morocco. It would be absurd, under the circumstances, for any Allied government to insist on the withdrawal of France from North Africa without insisting that Spain should withdraw also. This brings up the question of Spain itself. If Fascism is the chief menace to European peace, can it be left to fester and flourish in Spain? It would be ironical indeed if all the Fascist dictators who have fought so valiantly for the maintenance of the "new order" should be defeated, while General Franco, the least of them, should alone succeed, without fighting at all, in maintaining it. Well, it depends upon Russia, Great Britain, and the United States. A little pressure exerted by these powers, and General Franco would join Mussolini and Hitler in whatever limbo is reserved for them. Perhaps they will exert this pressure. Perhaps they will do after the war is over what they, supported by France, could and should have done before it began — "respect the right of all peoples to choose the form of government under which they will live."

4

The political settlement of Europe will thus depend in the first instance on the measures taken by the victorious powers — Russia, Great Britain, and the United States. Whether the settlement is as good as could be expected (it cannot in the nature of the case be entirely satisfactory to every country) depends partly on their ability to make a settlement that is equally satisfactory to them, and partly on the extent to which a settlement satisfactory to them is in accord with the political and national interests and aspirations of the other nations concerned.

A somewhat similar, but less clearly defined, situation will exist in the Far East. The political settlement there will likewise depend very largely on the measures taken by the victorious powers. Assuming that Russia does not become involved in the war with Japan, the victorious powers will be China, Great Britain, and the United States. They will desire a settlement that will destroy the power of Japan, maintain peace and order, and safeguard their own interests. But this will make it necessary to take into account other interests than their own — the interests of the dependent people of the Far East, notably the people of India, and the interests of certain European countries, such as France, Holland, and notably Russia. Since Great Britain and the United States will be closely associated with France and Holland in the European settlement, they cannot disregard the interests of Holland in the East Indies or those of France in Indo-China. Although Russia may not be directly concerned in making the peace with Japan, no settlement of the Far East can fail to take account of the fact that Russia is and will remain a major power in that part of the world. In that respect much will depend on whether Russia, Great Britain, and the United States are able to reach an agreement in the settlement of Europe. If they are, their relations in the Far East will be more friendly, but any serious conflict of interests in Europe will be an obstacle to the friendly adjustment of their interests in the Far East.

I am taking it for granted that Great Britain and the United States will retain, and probably increase, their naval and air power, and therefore their political power, in the Far East. One reason is that China will desire their continued co-operation and support. The Japanese, however completely defeated and disarmed, will remain a potential danger; and I should think the Chinese would feel much safer if British and American naval and air forces remain close at hand as a safeguard against future Japanese aggression.

However that may be, it is extremely unlikely that the people of the United States or of the British Commonwealth of Nations will think it desirable to "withdraw" from the Far East. Mr. Clarence Buddington Kelland is reported to have said that the Pacific must become "an American lake." This manifestation of the more stupid forms of German and Japanese mentality does not, I hope, fairly represent American public opinion; but it is safe to say that the people of the United States will not have fought a desperate war to maintain their inadequately guarded position in the Pacific and then think it sensible to abandon it. They will be far more apt to think it sensible to do what, if it had been done before the war began, would have made the war less desperate. That is to say, they will think it sensible to strengthen their position in the Pacific. It is likely that the Filipinos, whether granted the privilege of self-government or not, will think so too. It is certain that the Australians will. The Australians, for good or ill, are in the Far East. They are not, and in the nature of the case cannot be, a great power. They are a part of the British Empire and look to Great Britain for protection. Almost as much, if not more, they now look to the United States. For these reasons we may assume that Great Britain and the United States, whatever political freedom may be given to the Filipinos and the people of India, will remain as major powers in the Far East.

No country, however, will have so vital an interest in the settlement of the Far East as China. In certain respects the interests of China may be in conflict with those of Great Britain and the United States, but so far as Japan is concerned the three countries will no doubt agree well enough. They will agree that Japan must be completely defeated, disarmed, and rendered incapable, within any foreseeable future, of embarking on another war for conquest and domination. Japan will of course be required to withdraw from all Chinese or other territory occupied since the war began. China will also demand, according to a statement recently made by the Chinese Ambassador at Washington, that Korea be made independent and that Formosa be restored to the Chinese Republic. The Ambassador declined to commit himself, however, as to the demands of China in respect to Manchuria and Hong Kong, which probably means that China will ask the British to withdraw from Hong Kong, and will be willing to settle the question of Manchuria in a way that is, so far as possible, agreeable to Russia. As for Indo-China, the Ambassador said that China would make no claim to it. If that is so, a difficult situation will be avoided, since France will probably wish to recover Indo-China, and the importance of France in the European settlement will make it difficult for

Great Britain and the United States not to support her claims in the Far East. No such difficulty is likely to arise in respect to the Dutch East Indies, and if Holland desires to retain her possessions there, as she probably will, I should think it likely that Great Britain and the United States will be in favor of her demands, and China not opposed.

Prophecy is notoriously dangerous, and in respect to details much of what I have suggested is in the nature of speculation. But at all events whatever changes may be made in boundaries of countries and the forms of government established, the political structure of the world after the political settlement of Europe and the Far East is completed will be in essentials much the same as it was before the war. There will be, as before, a few great states and many minor and small states. The principal change will be that, for an indefinite future, Germany and Japan will not be great powers. The great powers will be Russia, Great Britain, the United States, and China in so far as China can make politically effective the resources of her people and country. In all states, except in Germany and Italy and perhaps in Japan, the form of government will be much the same as before; in each state, as before, individuals will follow their "interests," groups will exert their "pressure," and the government will be chiefly concerned with the problem of reconciling or compromising these interests and pressures. But each state will, as before, have a real or supposed "national interest," which it will endeavor to secure with whatever political power it can command; and from the resulting community or conflict of national interests there will arise a certain "balance of power" in Europe, in the two Americas, in the Near and the Far East, and in the world at large.

This, or something very like it, will be the political structure of the world after the preliminary settlement of Europe and the Far East is completed. Upon this political structure the new international order, if there is to be one, must be based. The responsibility for creating a new international order rests upon all individuals and all states; but the chief responsibility rests upon the people and governments of the United States, Great Britain, Russia, and China — the great, imperial, imperialist powers, call them what you like. The major responsibility falls to them because they will have the major power, and nothing new can be created unless they take the initiative in creating and maintaining it. Mr. Churchill has said that if the United States and Great Britain maintain their present intimate union, everything can be accomplished; if not, nothing can be accomplished. That is only partly true. It is certainly true that if the United States and the British Commonwealth of Nations cannot work together in harmony and good faith for the creation of a new international order, no new international order can be created. But it is also true that if they, although united, cannot work with Russia and China in harmony and good faith, the hope of a new international order is almost equally sure to be defeated.

This is generally admitted. But there seems to be a widespread belief that if these four great powers can maintain their present union, make a political settlement in Europe and the Far East that is in accord with the political and national interests and aspirations of the nations concerned, and then create some sort of "international machinery" for maintaining peace, or what the Atlantic Charter refers to as a "wider and permanent system of general security," all will be well — war will be prevented and the new order assured. To do even this much will be difficult enough, although not too difficult; and to do even this much would be to create a better international order than Germany and Japan would have created if they could have won the war. But to suppose that this would be enough to create an order essentially better than the one created after the last war, or different from it, is to be deceived.

What needs to be understood is that a *political* settlement, however necessary and however excellent, is not enough. The world will not be freed from "fear and want," from confusion and conflict, from aggression and war, merely because the great states "respect the right of all peoples to choose the form of government under which they will live," cease to be aggressive themselves, and "co-operate" through an "international organization," backed by an "international police force," to prevent aggression on the part of others. In the modern world political conflict and confusion, international aggression and war, are the results of an underlying economic confusion and conflict. A new and better world, in the national and the international realm, can be created only if and in so far as the essential causes of economic confusion and conflict are understood, and only if and in so far as the great and small states of the world are willing to unite in measures that are necessary if those causes are to be eliminated.

8

What Kind of International Economic Order Can We Have?

I HAVE DISCUSSED the political settlement first and by itself, but that does not mean that after the war is won representatives of the victorious powers will immediately sit around a peace table and work out, within a few months, a political settlement before concerning themselves with other matters. On the contrary, the immediate and most pressing problems which will confront the victorious powers will be essentially economic. The political settlement may well be long delayed, and its nature in some measure determined, by an economic situation the gravity of which no one can now foresee, but which will in any case be far more serious than the one that followed the last war.

When the Armistice was signed in November 1918, the only countries that had been conquered by Germany were Luxembourg and Belgium and some of the Balkan states, but even these countries had not been systematically looted, nor had their institutions been destroyed. Brief and almost bloodless revolutions occurred in Austro-Hungary and Germany, which resulted in the creation of several new states and the organization of new forms of government; but in

neither Germany nor the countries formerly compos-
ing the Austro-Hungarian Monarchy were the underlying economic, legal, or administrative institutions
essentially changed. Many countries were exhausted
and impoverished by the war, and it was necessary for
the Allied nations to provide food and other necessities for the people in many parts of Europe; but in
no European country was there anything that could
be called a complete collapse of economic and political
order.

The situation at the close of the present war will be
a far more serious one. Germany has conquered virtually all of continental Europe except Italy, Switzerland, Spain, and Portugal. All the conquered countries have been systematically looted. Their principal
banking and industrial corporations have passed to
German ownership or control. The private property
of millions of people has been confiscated, and vast
masses of the population have been displaced. In all
the conquered countries political and intellectual
leaders have been executed or forced into exile, and
political and legal institutions have been transformed
or destroyed. In by far the greater part of continental
Europe the only political authority, economic order,
or legal procedure that now exists is integrated with
the German Nazi regime and sustained by nothing
but the Nazi power. When Germany is defeated the
Nazi regime will collapse, and the only political authority, economic order, or legal procedure there is
in the greater part of Europe will for the time being
disappear. The result, so far as one can now foresee,
will be a condition of political and economic chaos,
of hunger and desolation, of embittered hatreds and

reprisals such as Europe has not known since the Thirty Years' War.

The collapse of the Nazi system in Europe may be quite sudden or spread out over many months. In any case the occupying forces will have to deal with the situation created by it. The reconquest of North Africa and Sicily gives us some slight idea of what will need to be done. But the situation in these regions was much simpler than it is likely to be in Germany, or in the countries conquered by Germany and for four years subjected to the Nazi exploitation and terror. The immediate task in any case will be to provide food for the destitute, establish administrative order, and prevent individual or mass reprisals. A more difficult and prolonged task will be to supervise the revival of economic life — to get the people back to some degree of normal agricultural and industrial production. A great deal of capital and an extended organization will be needed for all this — for feeding the hungry, arranging for the return of displaced populations, and replacing worn-out and providing new equipment for farms, industrial plants, transportation systems, and the like. There will be, in short, the stupendous task of demobilizing the Nazi "new order" in Europe, military and civil, and restoring some sort of orderly peacetime living. One has only to think of the incredible devastation of Poland to have some dim idea of what that task will be like.

Not the least difficult although not the most immediately pressing task will arise in connection with confiscated property. The Germans have confiscated, by forced sale of land and other real estate, or by carrying off food, livestock, and industrial equipment, property to the value of some billions of dollars belonging to private persons, corporations, or governments in the conquered countries. It is generally agreed that Germany must restore this property or pay for it. The original owners will in any case present claims for losses, but what means will there be for determining whether the contract sales were forced or genuine, or whether the claims presented are correct? It is said that in Czechoslovakia and Poland the original registers of land titles have been destroyed. The movable property carried out of the conquered countries has been used up and cannot be restored, and Germany will not be able to pay for it at once. So far as equipment is needed for immediate economic recovery, the victorious powers must provide for it.

It is not, however, merely a question of tangible property. When it is said that Germany has "looted the conquered countries" we are apt to form a picture of trucks and freight trains carrying off into Germany immense quantities of food, livestock, household goods, farm machinery, the equipment of industrial plants, the contents of art galleries and museums, and the like. The picture is correct enough, but the Germans have found other and more effective means of looting the conquered countries than that. The most effective means has been through the control of banks and the manipulation of financial operations. In France, for example, the Bank of France floated loans which were subscribed to by the French people. The money thus accumulated was turned over by the controlled Vichy government to Germany. With this money the Germans then bought French property and securities, paying the owners in depreciated French currency. This money the owners invested in French government bonds, and the money thus obtained was again turned over to Germany. Thus, as has been well said, "the French were made to finance their own destruction." [1] The same methods were used in other countries; and although the property values thus confiscated can never be fully determined, the complicated integration of European banks and corporations with the German banks will have to be unscrambled and innumerable claims examined and adjusted.

These are some of the economic problems that will arise after the collapse of the Nazi power in Europe. If they were left to the unorganized people of Europe to deal with, the result would be a prolonged period of impoverishment, destitution, and civil conflict. Only with the aid and supervision of the victorious countries during an indefinite period of military occupation can the necessary measure of economic order be restored. For reasons of interest as well as of humanity it will be necessary for the victorious countries to provide this aid and supervision. Even for strictly political reasons, for enabling the people of Germany and the conquered countries to establish responsible governments, it will be necessary. It is all very well to say that the German and other nations will be permitted to "choose the form of government under which they will live." But it is obvious that this cannot be done so long as the economic life of the people is in a state of confusion. We are apt to form a picture of the various peoples of Europe, within a few months after the collapse of the Nazi power, going to the polls

[1] *New York Times,* quoted in Frank Munk: *The Legacy of Nazism* (New York: The Macmillan Company; 1943), p. 132.

in an orderly manner to "express the will of the people" by voting for organized political parties with well-known leaders and well-defined party programs. The picture is pure fancy. For four years all the old parties have been dissolved, their leaders have been driven into hiding or exile, their means of forming and expressing opinion have been destroyed. No one can even imagine what drastic changes four years of war and social dislocation will have brought about. It is unlikely that in any conquered country, it is especially unlikely that in Germany, "the will of the people," except in the sense that they long for "freedom," can be expressed until after a considerable lapse of time — time for the restoration of some measure of economic order, time for getting adjusted to the new situation, time for new leaders to arise, new parties to be formed, new programs to be set forth and discussed and accepted. In short, time for the disorganized nation to find out what the situation is and to make up its mind what to do about it.

No one can now foresee how long this will take, or what new leaders and parties will emerge, or what modification of the pre-war forms of government the various peoples of Europe will be in favor of. The answer to such political questions depends very much on the economic situation; and it is at this point that the political and the economic settlements are related. In Germany, for example, what is to be done with the financial and industrial power now concentrated in the interrelated corporations known as the Hermann Goering Works? Political democracy in Germany depends very much upon whether the Hermann Goering Works, or some similar form of entrenched financial and industrial power, is permitted to survive. Likewise in France. Are the pre-war banking and industrial corporations, and the power they commanded, to be restored to their original owners? Pre-war democracy in France, in which the industrial and financial classes thought "Socialism" a greater danger than Nazism, and the working classes thought the war a "rich man's war" and no concern of theirs, was a pretty sad and corrupt and feeble thing. Anything less corrupt and feeble, or more disposed to co-operate in creating a new international order, will require some drastic changes in the economic system. The political settlement in each country is thus inseparable from the economic settlement.

The same is true of the international political settlement: whether it amounts to anything depends upon what measures are taken to solve fundamental economic problems. Let the United States, Great Britain, Russia, China, and the minor states "co-operate" with the best will in the world. Let them set up whatever political league, federation, or "international machinery" they like, backed by whatever "international police force" they think necessary. They will still find that to prevent war and aggression, to abolish "fear and want," it will be necessary to eliminate their causes. They will find that to eliminate their causes it will be necessary to do more than get rid of a bunch of "war-breeding gangsters." They will find that it is necessary to deal with such matters as international trade and investments, currency stabilization, the development of industrially backward countries, varying standards of living in the several countries, and access "on equal terms" to the raw materials of the world needed by each country. But such problems cannot even be intelligently discussed, much less solved, without taking into account the measures adopted in each country for dealing with full production and unemployment, tariffs, foreign investments, currency regulation, the control of patents and the activities of corporations involved in international cartels, and the like. If there is to be a new and better world, the international economic order no less than the national economic order must be more or less planned; and national and international economic problems are so intimately related that planning in either field cannot very well succeed unless it is in some measure integrated with planning in the other.

It is certain, however, that the several countries will retain control of their several national economies, however much or little planned. It is certain that no country, the more powerful countries least of all, will be willing to turn over the control of its national economic arrangements to any independent international organization. The possibility of a new international economic order depends, therefore, on the disposition and the ability of the people and governments of the several countries — above all, of the more powerful countries — to work together, through such political and economic international agencies as may be necessary, to adjust their several national economies for the solution of concrete international economic problems as they arise. Out of such co-operative effort, and only so in my opinion, is there much chance for the gradual creation of any new international order, political or economic.

Of the many long-time concrete economic problems

which will arise after the preliminary peace settlement is completed, and which will need to be in some measure solved before a new international order can emerge, none is more frequently mentioned in current discussions of post-war reconstruction than the "revival of international trade." But why will it need to be "revived"? Why will it not revive of its own accord?

1

Before 1914 there was little talk about reviving international trade. There was no occasion for it, because international trade for the most part went on very well without any assistance. The nineteenth century, when the new inventions and power-driven machines were being introduced, was a period of rapid industrial and commercial expansion — a golden age of business enterprise and material prosperity. And for no country more so than for Great Britain. Great Britain was, so to speak, in on the ground floor, the first country to make extensive use of the new technology. During most of the century Great Britain was, therefore, the leading manufacturing, exporting, and creditor country of the world. Less highly industrialized countries — the United States and the countries of continental Europe — needed British manufactured goods, and they needed British capital for financing their industrial development — for building railroads and industrial plants, opening up mines, and the like. Great Britain, on the other hand, needed food and raw materials for her industries; and, realizing that she could not export goods and capital to other countries unless they were allowed to pay for them in food and raw materials, she adopted a policy of free trade. As long as this situation lasted, as long as Great Britain needed food and raw materials from the rest of the world, and the rest of the world needed British-manufactured goods and capital, the conditions for industrial expansion and thriving international trade were as nearly ideal as they are ever likely to be.

Towards the end of the nineteenth century the conditions became less ideal. By that time the United States, Germany, France, and other European countries to a less extent, had also become manufacturing countries. They had also accumulated capital. They too, like Great Britain, had manufactured goods to sell to other countries, and capital of their own seeking investment abroad. All these countries therefore began to compete with Great Britain for the sale of manufactured goods, the investment of capital abroad, and the control of regions where essential raw materials for industry, such as oil and rubber, were to be had. The result was what is called the "new imperialism" — the competitive struggle of the industrialized countries of Europe and America for colonies, "spheres of influence," "concessions," and the like in the "backward countries"; that is to say, the industrially undeveloped countries of the world — Africa, Turkey, Persia, and the Far East. For some twenty-five years this competitive scramble went on without giving rise to serious difficulty. But at the turn of the century (1898–1904) there were ominous signs of coming disaster — the little "colonial wars," the Spanish American War, the Boer War, the "Boxer Rebellion" in China, the Russo-Japanese War. And then the disaster itself, the World War of 1914–18, which marked the end of a century of unprecedented industrial expansion, thriving international trade, and material prosperity.

During this century business expansion and international trade were facilitated by the general adoption of the "gold standard." That is to say, the chief countries adopted gold as the standard of value for their own money and for settling their trade balances. For a long time the relative values of the different money units remained fixed within narrow limits, so that anyone who sold or bought goods or invested capital abroad did not need to fear that within six months or six years he might suffer losses by the depreciation of foreign money values. He could count with great certainty on the American dollar being equal approximately to four English shillings, four German marks, five French francs, and so on. This was so long the case that most people took it for granted that it would always be so — provided, that is, the various countries maintained the gold standard, which it seemed fantastic to suppose they would not do. The gold standard became, in short, a kind of sacred cow in all economic thinking. It was regarded as one of the great inventions — a mechanism which had only to be installed to make the system of national and international trade self-regulating. Unfortunately, this was an illusion. It was putting the cart before the horse, taking the effect for the cause. International trade did not flourish because the gold standard was adopted; on the contrary, it was possible and convenient to use the gold standard because international trade was, and had long been, for other reasons, in a flourishing condition.

This became apparent after the first World War. The first World War, as Professor Jacob Viner says, "put an end to this monetary golden age." It put an end to the monetary golden age because it marked the end of the golden age of business and commercial expansion which made the gold standard possible and convenient. In the 1920's there had ceased to be the "conditions which are necessary for the smooth and beneficial working of an international metallic standard." Among these necessary conditions Professor Viner mentions "moderation in trade barriers, flexible price structures, and the initial establishment of exchange rates consistent with maintenance of equilibrium in international balance payments without resort to seriously deflationary measures at home." Since these necessary conditions no longer existed,

the gold standard of the 1920's was a fragile thing. . . . It maintained a precarious existence largely with the aid of the infusion of dollar credits by gullible — and gulled — American investors, individual and institutional. Its weakness became apparent with the cessation of American export of capital in 1929, and its collapse began almost immediately after the first onslaught of the great depression. England . . . abandoned it in a violent manner in 1931. The United States abandoned it in an even more violent manner in 1933. In 1936, with the unduly prolonged demise of the "gold bloc" — France, Belgium, Holland, and Switzerland — the gold standard survived apparently only in Albania.[1]

[1] *Yale Review*, Autumn 1943, p. 79.

This is to say that the various countries abandoned the gold standard because under the existing conditions it wouldn't work any more. Abandoning the gold standard was the result, not the cause, of profound dislocations in the system of international trade, and these were in turn the result of the Great Depression, which ended business expansion, created mass unemployment, and forced the governments of the various countries to take extraordinary measures for bringing about economic recovery. Every government realized that in order to bring about economic recovery at home it was highly desirable to revive international trade. But for the most part the measures taken to revive international trade ran counter to the measures taken to bring about economic recovery at home, and the measures taken to revive business expansion at home were obstacles to the revival of international trade. For example, in Great Britain and the United States the gold standard was abandoned because it seemed necessary in order to ease up the depression at home; and when these countries abandoned the gold standard, other countries were compelled to abandon it also for similar reasons. But going off the gold standard, without providing some other means of settling international balances, contributed to the further decline of international trade. It was not quite so simple as all that, of course; but in general most countries found that if they went in for regulating their domestic economies it was necessary to sacrifice a good deal in the way of foreign commerce.

The most obvious way in which the regulation of domestic economy and foreign trade are related is through tariffs levied on the importation of goods from abroad. Professor Viner mentions "moderation in trade barriers" as one of the necessary conditions for the smooth working of international exchanges — one of the favorable conditions which had ceased to exist in the 1920's. There was even less moderation in the 1930's; and in this respect the United States was the worst offender. Since 1815 the United States has always levied tariffs on imported goods. The policy is called "protection" as opposed to "free trade," for the reason that the original purpose of the tariff was to "protect infant industries" — industries that were just getting established — against competition from foreign industries using cheap labor. But the policy was continued even after the infant industries became giants capable of competing with the strongest; and although there have been a few tariff laws which lowered the rates, the general trend has been to raise the rates and increase the number of commodities protected.

In the nineteenth century there may have been good reasons for our tariff policy. But whether there were good reasons or not, the tariffs, even though high, did not seriously interfere with business or commercial expansion. One reason for this is that the United States was then what is called a "debtor country." This means that the interest on foreign capital invested in this country plus the cost of goods imported was greater than the value of goods which we exported abroad. For this and other reasons foreign countries found it profitable to sell goods in this country in spite of high tariffs. But since the first World War we have become the principal "creditor country" of the world. Our investments abroad have been enormous, and we have had more goods to sell abroad than we needed to buy abroad. If, under these conditions, we wished to extend our foreign markets the thing to do was to lower the tariffs so that foreign countries could afford to sell us more goods in payment for what we sold them. This simple fact was recognized by President Wilson even before the first World War; and for this and other reasons he got the Congress to enact the Underwood Tariff law in 1913 which abolished the tariff on some goods and lowered it on others.

This was certainly a wise policy even in 1913. After the first World War the wisdom of such a policy should have been even more obvious. Nevertheless the policy was abandoned in the 1920's; and in 1931, after the Great Depression, the Hawley-Smoot Tariff law was enacted. Of all American tariff laws, this one is now regarded by all the experts as the worst — that is to say, the most excessive in its rates, and the least well designed to promote even the selfish interests of those who clamored for it. The Hawley-Smoot Tariff made it still more difficult for foreign countries to sell us goods, and accordingly more difficult to pay for the goods which we wished to sell to them. It therefore contributed much to the collapse of international trade in the 1930's, and by offending nearly every important country in the world played its part in destroying whatever little amity and goodwill among nations there was left. It was based on the false assumption that the United States (or any other country) can sell goods and services to other countries without buying their goods and services in return; and one striking result of this error is that we now have about eighty per cent of the world's gold supply, a great part of which is buried in Kentucky and of no use to us or anyone else.

The experience of the 1930's seems to have demonstrated one fundamental truth — that if each country goes on its own and on the loose in the effort to revive business prosperity at home and promote its foreign trade it will not succeed very well in doing either. The collapse of business prosperity within the several countries, and the collapse of international trade between them, were merely different aspects of one complicated problem; and in the long run no country can arrive at any satisfactory solution of this problem, in either of its aspects, without taking into account what other countries are doing to achieve the same end. Fortunately, this is much better and more widely understood now than ever before. It has long been understood by economic experts, but the important point is that it is coming to be understood by responsible public officials. Evidence of this is to be found in respect to two specific measures, one of them tentatively adopted, the other proposed and more or less officially sanctioned by the governments of Great Britain and the United States. One of these is the tentatively adopted policy of the United States in dealing with tariffs; the other consists in the so-called Keynes and White plans for international currency stabilization.

Some four years ago the Congress authorized the President, through the Department of State, to revise tariff schedules by "reciprocal agreement" with the particular countries concerned. The authorization was limited to four years, but has now been extended for two years more. The procedure is somewhat as follows. If for any reason it seems desirable to revise the tariffs imposed by the United States on goods imported from any country — let us say Brazil — the matter is first considered at length by officials of both countries, with the object of finding out, if possible, what rates would be most satisfactory and advantageous to both countries. If an agreement can be reached, an opportunity is then provided for those American business interests that may be affected by the revised rates to examine them and to raise objections or offer suggestions. In the light of these objections and suggestions the schedule of rates is again considered, and if it seems desirable further revised, so that everyone concerned may be as well satisfied as possible. Something of this sort. The precise method of procedure for arriving at "reciprocal agreement" does not matter. What matters is the principle — the assumption that it is not to the interest of the United States to levy tariffs on imports from Brazil (or any other country) without taking into account the effect which those tariffs will have on the economic prosperity of Brazil, and as a consequence upon the attitude, friendly or hostile, of Brazil towards the United States. The general assumption is that international trade is a two-way street, and that the business prosperity and foreign trade of the United States cannot in the long run be best promoted by imposing tariffs on goods imported from other countries that will seriously injure the business prosperity and foreign trade of those countries.

The assumption is certainly a sound one. The policy tentatively adopted by the United States should be made permanent. If adopted as the settled policy of the United States it might well be adopted by many other countries; and if and when the chief countries realize that tariffs and trade barriers are matters of common interest, which cannot be settled to the best advantage by each country acting on its own, then there might well be established an international commission for making a scientific study of the problem in its international as well as in its national bearings, and for recommending those measures which would be most advantageous to all and several. This would be at least one approach to the solution of a definite, concrete international problem; and in so far as it proved successful it would at least be something solid achieved in the way of international co-operation, something practical accomplished in the way of creating a new international order.

But the question of international trade and "trade barriers" cannot be discussed intelligently, much less answered, without raising the central question of the stabilization of international exchanges. Most economic experts believe that a return to the gold standard is out of the question, and that accordingly some other means of stabilization must be devised. And in fact two specific plans for stabilization have been drafted — one by Harry White, the monetary adviser of the United States Treasury, the other at least chiefly by J. M. Keynes, for the British Treasury. Neither plan has been officially approved, but there is good reason for supposing that the White plan is the one which the American government prefers, and that the Keynes plan is the one which the British government prefers; and for this reason the White plan is commonly referred to as the "American plan," and the Keynes plan as the "British plan."

In certain respects the two plans are similar. Both plans provide for the creation of an international organization, called in the White plan the "United and Associated Nations Stabilization Fund," and in the Keynes plan the "International Clearings Union." In both plans any country is free to join the organization provided it meets the specified conditions. In both plans the organization is in the nature of an international bank, which does business, however, only with governments or authorized government agencies, such as treasuries. The primary object of both plans is to facilitate international trade by stabilizing international exchanges; and for this purpose both plans provide for certain restrictions on the member countries in the management of their several national currencies, and for transferring money or "credit" from the countries that have more than they need to any country which happens to be temporarily in need of such assistance in making its international payments. The two plans differ, however, very considerably in respect to the precise procedure to be followed in achieving these general objects. The merits and defects of the two plans, and the probable effect of their adoption, have been discussed at length by many economists, and with varying conclusions on their part — among others by Professor Peter F. Drucker in *Harper's Magazine* for July 1943, and Professor Jacob Viner in the autumn *Yale Review* of the same year. These two experts assess the merits and defects of the two plans somewhat differently; but they agree on the main point — the main point for this discussion — that some plan is necessary, and that both these plans are on the whole excellent. "The most encouraging feature of the Keynes and White plans," says Professor Drucker, "is that they agree, on the whole, on the diagnosis of the problem which international organization has to master." Professor Viner would prefer a "blend of the two" plans, but he is convinced that the "adoption of either plan very much as it now stands would be a great step forward, in the mutual interest of all countries wishing an orderly and collaborative world."

The precise merits and defects of these plans need not concern us. What chiefly concerns us is that both the British and the American governments have recognized the need of international co-operation in this important matter, have gone so far at least as to have definite plans drafted, and will very probably attempt to put into operation whatever "blend" of the Keynes and White plans they can agree upon. If they succeed in doing so, that will be another solid, concrete achievement in the way of creating a new international order.

But "monetary stabilization alone," as Professor Viner says, "will not suffice to cure the world of its troubles in the international economic field." Among many other things to be considered is the treatment to be accorded the so-called backward countries. Are they to be economically developed along the lines of Western industrial and technological civilization? If so, are they to be supplied with Western capital, and if so will the supply take the form of competitive exploitation or of co-operative international assistance?

225

This raises the vexed question of "imperialism" again, which is after all fundamentally an economic rather than a political problem.

2

The central difficulty in the problem of "imperialism" has been, I will not say elucidated, but at least unconsciously divulged by Mr. Lin Yutang in his recent book *Between Tears and Laughter.* Lin Yutang is an ardent Chinese patriot who has lived long enough in France, England, and the United States to become intimately acquainted with Western people and Western civilization. Western civilization alternately amuses and exasperates Mr. Lin. In itself, he likes Western civilization well enough — well enough at all events to endure living in it. What exasperates him is the Western man's settled conviction that his civilization is superior to that of China or India, and more especially his capacity to exploit the people of China and India for his own advantage and still believe that he is doing them a favor by bringing them the benefits of Western civilization.

About the "superiority" of Western civilization Mr. Lin has much to say, and says it with point and wit. He finds that Western civilization has some advantages. It has central heating, hot and cold shower baths, and the very best and cheapest soap. It has machines of infinite delicacy and power, capable of making or destroying anything in no time at all, and of carrying people with incredible speed from the place where they are to some other place, any other place, where they will in all likelihood be no better off than they were. Western civilization is based on mathematics, statistics, Diesel engines, and high explosives. It is the quintessence of activity pursued without direction and power employed without purpose. Chinese civilization has not these advantages, but it has something better. It has tranquillity and leisure — time to be polite and drink tea, time to look at a sunset, time to sit still and be content and reflect on the nature of man and the meaning of life. It does very well without mathematics and statistics. And so Mr. Lin says, no, thank you, the Chinese do not want Western civilization with all its excellent cheap soap and other blessings. The Chinese want only to be left alone with what they have, and to be judged on their merits as a great nation worthy of being treated on equal terms with any other.

This is what the Chinese want, but according to Mr. Lin this is what they will never have so long as they have not the power to exact it. And so it turns out, according to Mr. Lin, that the Chinese, although they do not want Western civilization, must nevertheless, in order to avoid being shoved around, acquire that part of Western civilization in which it is superior. They must acquire mathematics and statistics, clocks, Diesel engines, and high explosives. Only when they have more power than the white man will the white man think them as good as he is — or even a little better than he is, since 500,000,000 Chinese, fully equipped with warships and bombing planes will be no laughing matter. In the world created by the white man, 500,000,000 Chinese, fully equipped with mechanical and industrial power, could not possibly be wrong or inferior, or shoved around without more difficulty than it would be worth.

Well, Mr. Lin is quite right. He has, as I say, divulged the crucial difficulty in the problem of "imperialism." Whether Chinese civilization is in general superior to Western civilization, whether either is superior to ancient Greek civilization, I do not know. Maybe mankind would be better off if no tribe had ever emerged from the primitive state. But however that may be, it is a fact that the form which civilization takes has always been profoundly influenced by the technological instruments of power at man's disposal; and that since primitive men learned how to use a lever or control fire no kind of mechanical power once discovered has ever been voluntarily discarded. Western civilization may be inferior to Chinese civilization in many respects, but it is obviously superior in mechanical, and therefore in economic and political, power; and apart from the return of another "Dark Age" of ignorance, there is no possibility that the scientific knowledge and mechanical power upon which Western civilization is based will be abandoned. On the contrary, these aspects of Western civilization will in the future, as in the past, spread more widely throughout the world. Mr. Lin is right. In the world as it has been created by the white man the people of China and India must acquire the knowledge and the power which the white man commands. Like it or not, they must have his mathematics and statistics, his Diesel engines and high explosives, his hot and cold showers and excellent cheap soap — his machine technique and mass production that *can* abolish want and famine, and his medical science that *is* conquering disease and banishing pestilence.

But if India and China (and other economically

undeveloped countries) are to have these aspects of Western civilization — its mass production, scientific agriculture, methods of transportation, medical efficiency — how are they to get them? Hitherto, except in Japan, Western methods have, as one may say, filtered into the "backward" countries as an incidental result of Western "imperialistic" expansion. The evils of Western imperialistic expansion have often enough been pointed out; and certainly it cannot be said that Europeans and Americans have gone into Africa, China, and India, the East Indies and the Philippines for the laudable purpose of "civilizing and Christianizing" the native people, as President McKinley said, or in order to provide every child, as Henry Wallace desires, with his daily bottle of milk. This is admitted. Nevertheless, the white man's presence in the "backward" countries has not been, as is too often assumed, entirely injurious to the native peoples, and we ought to give the devil — even the devil of imperialism — his due.

Take, for example, India, about which so much is now being said to the discredit of the British. The British did not go into India to set up Sunday schools, but it should not be forgotten that they have, as a by-product of other enterprises, improved conditions in India in many ways. It should not be forgotten that before the British came to India it was no crime to kill an "untouchable," that young widows were commonly burned on the funeral pyres of their deceased husbands, that illiteracy and poverty were more widespread than they are now. It should not be forgotten that the British have abolished the continual internal wars; have introduced, often in spite of opposition inspired by native ignorance and superstition, rail-roads, reservoirs, irrigation systems, hospitals, and medical service; have abolished plagues and greatly reduced famines; have established a more equitable system of administering justice and a far greater degree of freedom of speech and the press than ever existed before. It should not be forgotten that the very idea of political freedom, for which Mr. Nehru and others are now so ardently contending, is a British importation and not a native product. It should not be forgotten that since the last war the British have moved, perhaps too slowly, in the direction of giving to India more privileges of self-government, and that they are prepared after the war (so far as I can discover; I am not a special correspondent capable of solving the "problem of India" after a six months' sojourn there) to give complete political independence to India as soon as the Indians themselves can construct a political organization that is sufficiently supported by the various factions to be willing to take over that responsibility.

These things should not be forgotten. But, for all that, it is still true that Western imperialistic expansion was not primarily inspired by the desire to benefit the people of the "backward" countries. It was the result of the expansive forces inherent in Western industrial and technological civilization — capital seeking investment abroad, business men looking for markets and new opportunities for profitable business enterprise, governments desiring to gain control of countries where essential raw materials were to be had. It was the importance of rubber that led to the expansion of Belgium in the African Congo, the natural flow of European capital that got the British into Egypt and the French into Morocco, the opportunity for industrial and commercial profit that got the Russians into Manchuria and the Germans into Kiaochow and the British and the Russians into Persia, and that induced all the "great powers," including the United States, to exact "treaty port" concessions from the Chinese government. This expansion of capital and business enterprise was not always a one-sided affair. Not infrequently the backward countries were as eager for Western capital and business enterprise as the Europeans were to provide them. The rulers of Egypt and Morocco and Turkey went around Europe soliciting European capital and the assistance of European industrial experts because they wanted, for one reason or another, to develop the economic resources and more or less "Westernize" the institutions of their respective countries. But however that may be, the spread of Western technology and industrial civilization in the "backward" countries was essentially the result of the inherent tendency of capitalistic enterprise to expand in any part of the world where there were favorable opportunities for business or commercial enterprise. In this sense the spread of Western civilization through the world was the incidental result of the competitive exploitation of economically undeveloped countries for private profit and national advantage.

From the point of view of morality, of equal rights for all nations, there is little to be said in defense of this kind of imperialism. It is well enough, then, to say that imperialism in this sense must end, and that the "white man must get out of the Far East." But that

231

desired end will not be attained by any amount of moral indignation, although moral indignation may help some, or by any number of official promises to be good in the future, although promises to be good are never perhaps entirely without effect. After the present war, capital will, presumably, accumulate, especially if the principal industrial countries realize the great aim of full production and full employment; and accumulated capital will, presumably, seek investment in those countries that need it. If Lin Yutang is right, China will need a great deal of capital. And if poverty and destitution and illiteracy are to be abolished in India and every child is to have his daily bottle of milk, if, in short, India is to have the industries, railroads, schools, and hospitals that are essential if that great country is ever to be a united nation capable of self-government — if all or any great part of this is to come to pass, India will need as much capital as China or perhaps even more.

But where is the necessary capital to come from? Obviously from Europe and America if the end is to be attained within any reasonable time, or the people of China and India are not to be, for a generation or more, reduced to an even lower standard of living than they have hitherto had. If it is to come from Europe and America, that means, for the immediate future, chiefly from the United States and the British Commonwealth of Nations, since Hitler and Mussolini between them have reduced the greater part of Europe to the condition of "backward countries" needing outside capital for their own rehabilitation. If, then, after the war, Western capital again flows into China and India and the islands of the Seven Seas, if Western

232

business men again find opportunities in these countries for private profit, and if Western governments
are again disposed to safeguard the "national interest"
acquired as a result of the expansion of capital and
business enterprise — if this occurs again, it will be
useless to slap business men and governments on the
wrist and say: "Naughty, naughty; that is imperialism, and imperialism must be ended." If India and
China and other backward countries of the world are
to be industrialized by Western capital and business
enterprise and engineering skill, and yet not by the
old method of competitive struggle for private profit
and national advantage, then some better method
must be devised. Any better method could only be devised by co-operative international planning, through
some international agency; and the method would be
a better one only if the international agency should
have as its primary object the regulation and control of
capital investment in backward countries in such a
way as to eliminate the competitive struggle for private
profit and outside political control, and to make the
investment equally advantageous to the lending and
to the borrowing countries.

The international regulation of investments in
backward countries could hardly be divorced from the
regulation of foreign investments in general; nor could
foreign investments be regulated to good purpose
without taking into account many other matters.
Among these would be international trade and tariffs,
access to essential raw materials, international cartels,
stabilization of national currencies and international
exchanges, labor conditions, and the standard of living in the various countries. It is obviously to the in-

terest of each country to have as high a standard of living for its people as possible. Rightly considered, it is to the interest of each country that the standard of living in other countries should also be as high as possible. It is, for example, decidedly to the interest of Great Britain and the United States that the people of India and China should be prosperous and have a high standard of living, if Great Britain and the United States wish to invest great amounts of capital in those countries or wish to export great amounts of goods to them. But the question of a high standard of living for China and India and other countries at once raises the question, among others, of the world's food-supply and its proper distribution.

At present the world's food-supply is not sufficient to provide all the people of the world an adequate diet. However, if the resources, man power, and scientific knowledge available in the world were fully employed, it could be greatly increased — sufficiently so, at all events, to banish the starvation and undernourishment that exist in limited regions in nearly every country and are widespread and disastrous in Africa and Asia. But food is not now produced in order to meet the world's need for food, but either for the producer's own needs or to be sold by him at a profit; and virtually every food-producing country in the world has adopted measures designed to benefit the farmers as business men, rather than to get the maximum production of food that is necessary if no one is to go hungry. Under the competitive price system, it is to the advantage of farmers as business men that the price of farm products should be high; and in times of business contraction the easiest way to keep farm prices high seems to be to restrict production. The pre-war New Deal is a good example of this policy. With millions of people undernourished, the production of corn and wheat was cut down in order to raise the price to a point where it would be profitable for farmers to raise any corn or wheat at all. Obviously the problem of the world's food-supply and proper distribution cannot be solved by such a policy. You cannot provide the people of the world with the food they need by cutting down the production of food in every food-producing country.

It was perhaps a realization of this obvious fact that led President Roosevelt to call the recent international Food Conference at Hot Springs, which was attended by 360 delegates from forty-four countries. The matters discussed, the aims formulated, and the difficulties encountered at this conference have been summarized and made the basis of an admirable analysis of the subject by Mr. C. Hartley Grattan in *Harper's Magazine* for August 1943. The conference found no difficulty, of course, in formulating the grand general object, which is simply to provide all the people of the world with the food they need. The secrecy in which the proceedings of the conference were veiled did not extend to the point of refusing to inform us that "All men on earth are consumers of food." But it hardly needed 360 delegates from the ends of the earth to tell us that. What we might reasonably have expected the conference to do was to suggest some specific measures for providing all men on earth with food to consume. But the conference apparently found this very vital matter too hot to handle, and the reason is that any effective measures for attaining the general object would necessarily interfere with the present policy of restricting either the amount of food produced or its importation from foreign countries.

For political reasons none of the delegates, including those from our own country, could afford to do anything with this most vital but most embarrassing question except to leave it alone. This fact the conference announced in the following terms:

The prime responsibility lies with each nation for seeing that its people have the food needed for health and life: steps for this end are for national determination.

The grand result of the conference was thus to outline the problem and side-step its solution. Its failure to suggest any solution merely confirms the obvious fact that the problem of the world's food-supply and proper distribution is an international one, and that the steps to be taken for its solution are not for national but for international determination.

An international conference on raw materials for industry would meet with the same difficulty, since food, rightly considered, is itself an essential raw material for life, and therefore, one might suppose, for industry too. At all events the problem of raw materials is essentially the same as the food problem. It is, as the Atlantic Charter says, to assure to all nations "access, on equal terms, to the . . . raw materials of the world which are needed for their economic prosperity." As in the case of food, the end to be attained is easily stated, the means of attaining it difficult to determine, and, as in the case of food, the difficulties are chiefly political. It is obvious that the countries that have plenty of oil or rubber, for example, have an advantage, which they wish to keep, over those that have none. It is obvious that countries which have no oil or rubber, and even those which do, have an interest in controlling the regions of the earth where oil and rubber are or may be found. It is obvious that corporations which make their profit out of oil and rubber are not interested in providing all nations "access, on equal terms" to the oil and rubber of the world which are needed for their economic prosperity. They are interested in selling oil and rubber throughout the world at a price which will net them the greatest profit; and for this purpose they enter into agreements, or "cartels," with corporations in foreign countries which may, and often do, have the effect of limiting the production, fixing the price, and thereby determining the distribution of oil and rubber among the nations of the world.

A less well-known raw material than oil and rubber is tin. The largest tin deposits in the world are in the East Indies, the next largest are in Bolivia, a small inland South American country with a population of about three million, about ninety per cent Indians reduced to a state of virtual serfdom. This is so largely because the prosperity of Bolivia at present depends almost entirely on the tin industry, and the tin industry is controlled by the Patiño family. The Patiño family is said to be worth from half a billion to a billion dollars. Its income from Bolivia alone is greater than the revenue collected by the Bolivian government, and its political influence is such that it is said, correctly enough, that "Bolivia is Patiño." The Patiños' control of Bolivian tin is exercised through the Patiño Mines and Enterprises, Inc., which is incorporated in the state of Delaware. This company (or the Patiños as chief stockholders) controls General Tin Investments, Inc., of Great Britain, which in turn owns thirty-five per cent of the stock in British Tin Investments Corporation, which in turn has a large interest in thirty tin-mining concerns in Malaya. Simon Patiño and his son Antenor, through their interests in these various corporations, are "the strongest single power in the mining, smelting, and refining of tin, and hence the strongest power in the International Tin Cartel. The Cartel determines the amount each country in the world may produce [or did before the Japanese got Malaya]. What it says about the world price goes." [1] The Patiños have not lived in Bolivia for many years. They live in a luxurious suite in the Waldorf Astoria Hotel in New York. From that high vantage they can more or less arbitrarily determine how "free from want" or near the edge of starvation the people of Bolivia shall be, and what access and on what terms the nations of the world shall have to the tin which is "needed for their economic prosperity."

What could an international conference on raw material recommend as a remedy for a situation like this? What measures could Mr. Roosevelt or Mr. Churchill propose for freeing the Bolivian people from want, for enabling them to "choose the form of government under which they will live," or for assuring all nations access, on equal terms, to the tin that is needed for their economic prosperity? Nothing effective, certainly, without recommending drastic restraints on

[1] Carleton Beals: "Inside the Good Neighbor Policy," in *Harper's Magazine,* August 1943. The above information is taken from this article.

238

the tin czars Patiño and their corporations; and certainly neither Mr. Roosevelt nor Mr. Churchill would be in any position to recommend a drastic regulation of the Patiños unless they were prepared at the same time to recommend a similar regulation of British and American corporations which form similar cartels for similar purposes. It is obvious that the problem of raw materials and their proper distribution can be solved only by international agreement, and only by imposing drastic restraints, internationally agreed upon and enforced, on the activities of corporations and cartels of which the Patiño Tin Cartel is merely one example.

3

Such are some of the long-time economic problems that will have to be in some measure solved if there is to be a new international order. For if the world returns to the pre-war system of national economic isolation and conflict, a league, a federation, or political alliances will be of little avail since they will have no more secure foundation than they have had in the past. Responsibility for the solution of these international economic problems rests with all nations, but the chief responsibility rests with the people of the United States, the British Commonwealth of Nations, and Russia, and with China so far as China can make effective her potential political power. It rests with them because they will have the major political power. They cannot give up their political power. They can use it wisely or unwisely, for good ends or bad; they can lose it by social and economic disintegration or the disintegration of national sentiment and political unity; but they cannot give it to any other people or transfer it to any artificially created international political organization. They alone can use the power they have, and they alone are responsible for the use they make of it.

The responsibility rests chiefly with these four powers, but the initiative rests with the United States and the British Commonwealth of Nations rather than with China or Russia. With them rather than with China because China, although deeply concerned for the solution of these economic problems, will in all likelihood be for some time too impoverished and politically disordered to take the lead in solving them. With them rather than with Russia because Russia is less deeply concerned for the solution of these economic problems than the other countries are. The Russians will be in a position to say, and will in any case think: "The problem of unemployment and full production does not trouble us; we have already solved that problem; and it is because you, the capitalist democracies, have failed to solve it that you have to worry about international trade, foreign investments, the stabilization of international exchanges, and the imperialistic exploitation of backward countries." For these and other reasons it is for the United States and Great Britain to take the initiative. If they do not start something, no other countries will, and if they do not make a beginning nothing will be done.

But if nothing can be done unless the United States and Great Britain take the initiative, not much can be done unless Russia and China and many other countries join with them in the co-operative effort to attain the ends desired. These many countries must, then, be associated in some sort of union, however loose and flexible it may be. It would, however, I think, be a mistake to begin by blueprinting the union, defining beforehand the precise obligations of its members. It would be better to begin with an attempt to act together for solving a few immediate and pressing concrete problems, and let the union take whatever form may be found best suited for dealing with these and other problems as they arise. Let us not, then, irritate national egoism or offend the pride of sovereignty by inaugurating the union with flourish of trumpets, impressive ceremonies, and pledges given and taken for all future time. All of the words, resolutions, pledges, binding treaties, and solemn covenants that might conceivably induce the nations of the world to co-operate for the creation of a new and better world were uttered after the last war. What is needed is something less edifying and more prosaic, something less noisy but more effective. The contemplated union, league, federation, or whatever it is to be, will have a better chance of success if it begins, so to speak, "unbeknownst to itself," if it begins without declaring, or even professing to know, what nations may ultimately belong to it, or what the precise rights and obligations of its members may turn out to be. It will have a better chance of success, in short, if it begins without knowing or too much caring what it may become — if it begins with the drafting of specific agreements between a few or many nations for dealing with specific problems, and the creation of whatever international commissions, boards, agencies, may seem best suited for dealing with the specific problem in hand.

There would be nothing new or alarming in such

a procedure. The creation of international agencies or commissions is a familiar and long-established practice. The League of Nations is only the most striking and spectacular and widely heralded example of such international agencies; and much confusion of thought and much acrimonious denunciation of the League have arisen because of the mistaken notion that it was, or could be, something else. All the emphasis has been placed on the League as an international organization capable of preventing any war at any time and in any place. In this it failed. But few people seem to know that the League succeeded in so far as it acted strictly as an international agency for dealing with specific problems. Stripped of its war-prevention apparatus, the League consists of a number of permanent boards or commissions; and for twenty-five years these fact-finding commissions have been useful agencies of the member states for dealing with such concrete matters as labor relations, illicit traffic in narcotics and prostitution, and other matters which from time to time have been turned over to them.

In this respect the League of Nations is a going concern, although the name is no doubt misleading and too pretentious; and whatever new commissions or agencies may be created might well be centered in the League. If there is to be an international "Stabilization Fund" or "Clearings Union," if there are to be other international commissions for dealing with tariffs, capital investment in backward countries, the world's food-supply and proper distribution, they might well be a part of the Geneva setup. In so far as these experimental efforts to deal co-operatively

with specific problems prove successful or otherwise, the various agencies, commissions, boards could
be modified, abolished, expanded, or correlated as
seemed desirable. An international union begun in
this tentative way, and operating by these famil·
iar means, might conceivably accomplish something
worth while; whether much or little would depend on
the shape of things to come. Such a union would be
less in the nature of a created mechanism than a de-
veloping organism. It would at any time be what it
could be effectively used for doing, and would ultimately become, in form and procedure, what seemed
best suited to accomplishing the ends desired — the
promotion of the common interests of its members and
the preservation of amity and peace among them. In so
far as such a union succeeded in accomplishing these
ends, it would imperceptibly acquire "power," and as
it acquired power, nationalism would no doubt be imperceptibly abated and the independence of sovereign
states imperceptibly curbed.

That result is for the indefinite future. Making a
new and better world is a difficult business and will
prove to be a slow one. It is a matter of solving in some
measure two related and complicated problems. One
is the problem of abating the social conflict within nations, the other is the problem of abating the economic
and political conflict between them. Both problems
are fundamentally economic, and neither can be considered to good purpose without taking the other into
account. The end to be achieved, so far as it can be,
is to bring about full employment of man power, full
employment of technical and industrial productive
power, full development of the natural resources of

every country, and a proper distribution of the potential wealth of the world among men and nations. "International organization in the post-war period seems to imply," as Harold Laski says, "the need for the planned development of a world regarded as a common pool of wealth to which all nations have access, on terms as nearly equal as we can make them. The administration of the common pool needs common principles of action. Clearly enough, those common principles are the valuations of a new civilization." [1]

This is admittedly an ideal, incapable of being fully realized within any foreseeable future. But it is necessary to know what the ideal is in order to know what directions our effort should take; and much must be attempted in order that a little may be gained. Certainly nothing can be gained without knowing what we want and planning for it. It is no longer a question of planning or not planning, but a question of good, bad, or indifferent planning; and the essential point is that no plan for a new international world can succeed unless it is in some fashion integrated with measures taken in the principal countries for the organization of a new and better social world.

Making a new and better world is something that is, or should be, always going on. In the present state of the world the task is far more complex, and therefore far more difficult, than it has been for some centuries past; our only advantage is that we have more knowledge and more power for doing what needs to be done. If the war shocks us into taking the task more seriously than we have hitherto done, so much the better.

[1] *Reflections on the Revolution of Our Time,* p. 248.

But let no one suppose that the war will have made the task any easier, or have revealed to us any magic formula for setting the world straight all at once. Neither human nature nor fixed habits of thought nor social folkways can be wholly transformed within a single generation. Making a new and better world after the war will be what it always has been, a slow and dearly earned conquest of some additional and better-secured freedoms — the very freedoms which for countless generations men have longed for and with immense effort have in part won. If we can vindicate the dead and provide hope for the living we shall have done our share.

One hundred and fifty years ago, addressing those who were then engaged in making a new and better world, Edmund Burke said:

Society is indeed a contract. Subordinate contracts, for objects of mere occasional interest, may be dissolved at pleasure; but the state ought not to be considered as nothing better than a partnership agreement in a trade of pepper and coffee, calico or tobacco . . . to be taken up for a little temporary interest, and to be dissolved by the fancy of the parties. It is to be looked on with other reverence; because it is not a partnership in things subservient only to the gross animal existence of a temporary and perishable nature. It is a partnership in all science; a partnership in all art; a partnership in every virtue, and in all perfection. As the ends of such a partnership cannot be obtained in many generations, it becomes a partnership not only between those who are living, but between those who are living, those who are dead, and those who are to be born.[1]

[1] *Reflections on the French Revolution.*

With those who are dead we have maintained this partnership by cherishing what they have bequeathed to us. With those who are living we are maintaining it by fighting to preserve our inheritance from destruction. With those who are to be born we shall maintain it if, besides passing this legacy on to them, we can make such additions to its accumulated store of knowledge and wisdom as our generation is capable of producing.

Index

i

Index

This book was set on the Linotype in Baskerville. The punches for this face were cut under the supervision of George W. Jones, an eminent English printer. Linotype Baskerville is a facsimile cutting from type cast from the original matrices of a face designed by John Baskerville. The original face was one of the forerunners of the "modern" group of type faces.

Typography by W. A. Dwiggins. Binding design by Hollis Holland. Composed, printed, and bound by The Plimpton Press, Norwood, Massachusetts.